Earthing the Cosmic Queen

Earthing the Cosmic Queen

Relevance Theory and the Song of Songs

YAEL KLANGWISAN

With a Foreword by Tim Meadowcroft

☙PICKWICK *Publications* • Eugene, Oregon

EARTHING THE COSMIC QUEEN
Relevance Theory and the Song of Songs

Copyright © 2014 Yael Klangwisan. All rights reserved. Except for brief quotations in critical publications or reviews, no part of this book may be reproduced in any manner without prior written permission from the publisher. Write: Permissions, Wipf and Stock Publishers, 199 W. 8th Ave., Suite 3, Eugene, OR 97401.

Pickwick Publications
An Imprint of Wipf and Stock Publishers
199 W. 8th Ave., Suite 3
Eugene, OR 97401

www.wipfandstock.com

ISBN 13: 978-1-62564-499-2

Cataloging-in-Publication data:

Klangwisan, Yael

    Earthing the cosmic queen : relevance theory and the song of songs / Yael Klangwisan ; with a foreword by Tim Meadowcroft.

    xxiv + 152 pp. ; 23 cm—Includes bibliographical references.

    ISBN 13: 978-1-62564-499-2

    1. Bible. Song of Solomon—Criticism and interpretation. 2. Cohesion (linguistics). 3. Pragmatics. 4. Relevance (Philosophy). 5. Semantics. I. Meadowcroft, T. J. II. Title.

BS1485.53 K516 2014

Manufactured in the USA

The cover image, "Shulamith," by Ruth Bioletti, 2013.

English translations of the Hebrew Bible (apart from the Song of Songs) are from Tanakh: *The Holy Scriptures: The New JPS Translation According to the Traditional Hebrew Text.*

แด่ ชาญ

ฉันออกไปที่สวนขนุน
    เพื่อดูความชุ่มฉ่ำของกระแสธาร
    เพื่อดูมังคุดที่กำลังผลิช่อใบ
    เพื่อดูดอกมะม่วงที่กำลังคลี่บาน
    และก่อนที่ฉันจะรู้ว่าอะไรเป็นอะไร
    ฉันก็พบตัวเองอยู่บนหลังช้างเผือก!
    .....กับเจ้าชายผู้สูงศักดิ์...

ฉันไม่เคยลืมวันเวลาเหล่านั้น ครั้งแรกที่อีสาน,
เสียงเพลงของว่าวธนูต้องลม, ผลไม้แสนอร่อย,
ความอบอุ่น, สายลมแรง,
บรรยากาศที่อบอวลด้วยกลิ่นหอมของดอกมะลิ
สิ่งเหล่านี้ทั้งหมดเพื่อคุณ

    แรงบันดาลใจของฉัน...

        เจแอล

I don't go just to any strange Dreams. I go to those that resemble the ancient gardens where I spent a forgotten life, to those that spread out beneath the earth, before names, in the zones where music is spoken, where the languages before languages resound.

—Hélène Cixous

Contents

List of Figures and Tables   ix

Foreword by Tim Meadowcroft   xi

Preface   xv

Acknowledgments   xvii

Introduction   xix

1   *Pardes*: A Framework   1
    Old Fruits to New
    Relevance Theory
    Biblical Interpretation
    Pardes: The Essence of Communication

2   *Peshat*: A Discourse Analysis   29
    The Theoretical Framework
    The Text
    Translation
    Provenance
    Discourse Structure
    The Discourse Analysis
    Reading *Peshat* with the Poet

3   *Remez-Derasha*: Tracing the Contextual Environment   112
    The Garden
    Love for Love's Sake
    Liberating the Feminine

Contents

- Liberating Desire and Eating Fruit
- Liberating the Masculine
- Image of God and the Garden-Temple
- One Flesh
- Sleeping and Awaking
- Dressing and Undressing
- Aloneness
- Of Gardens, Cities, and Shalom
- A Message of Life

Conclusion   143

Bibliography   147

Figures and Tables

Figures

1. The initial discourse thread around the imagery of "rest" 9
2. Discourse analysis for verses 1:1–6 39
3. Questions asked by the daughters of Jerusalem 68
4. References to "mother" in the Song of Songs 109
5. Images of sleep and waking in the Song of Songs 134

Tables

1. Comparison of Egyptian *wasf* "The Stroll" and Song 4:1–5 52
2. Comparison of Gen 2:21 and Song 7:7–12 116

Foreword

"At sundry times and in divers manners" God spoke to our ancestors in the faith, according to the writer of the book of Hebrews (Heb 1:1), as rendered by the Authorised Version. At one time, and by means of one of those "divers manners," God surprisingly spoke in an erotic poem between two young people urgently in love with one another, apparently as physically engaged with each other as it is possible for a man and woman to be (4:16—5:1!), and deliberately heedless of anything that might confine or constrain the expression of their love, including—in that patriarchal society—any hint that their relationship might be other than mutual and egalitarian. And, however much sober commentators wish it otherwise, there is no mention by them of marriage.

What are we to do with this, those of us who read the Song of Songs today as part of a collection of texts through which we expect to hear God speak? The title of this book gives people like me a broad clue. That the "cosmic queen" is "earthed" reminds me of two important matters when approaching the Song. First, this is an earthy poem about everyday lived experience, partly because of the entrenched bucolic imagery that drives it and partly because it reflects that aspect of human experience which, more than any other, reminds us of and attracts us towards our physical embodiment as central to who we are. Secondly, that the Song should be "earthed" is a gentle reminder to us from Klangwisan to read it first on its own terms, and not merely as a pointer to some less physical and hence less dangerous reality, or as a metaphor of something else. In any case, if the Song does have a significance beyond itself, then this can hardly be glimpsed if the bodily experience of the Song itself is not fully entered into by the reader.

Yet this earthing is of something or someone named by Klangwisan as the "cosmic queen." To think first of the word "cosmic" by means of a change of medium, a good piece of art draws those who view it to wonder

Foreword

about the life outside the art itself. In his "Ode on a Grecian Urn," John Keats ponders the lives and significance of the "men or gods" and "maidens loth" depicted on the urn, wondering what their mission, caught in process at a moment of time, may have been. In that still moment he sees a group "For ever panting and for ever young," but in the very act of doing so looks forward (with foreboding, in the case of Keats) to the unknowable conclusion of their chase or consummation of their passion.

This phenomenon is also evident in the reading process. We may articulate the location of meaning in a text encountered in various ways: as the intention of the author; or the response of the reader; or the interaction of the two with the text itself. Yet, however we do so—unless the text encountered is so embedded in our experience and cultural context as to have moved beyond wonder—there is a deep-seated something within the reader that yearns to know more of the writer than is necessarily revealed. The story or poem itself may be of life within the world of the text, but it cannot help but pique curiosity of a life just outside the text. The Song of Songs does this in various ways. At one level it does so by means of its allusive poetic nature, which constantly evokes but never quite describes. It does so also as a participant in the collective known as the canon of Scripture. As a result we cannot escape a sense that, while the Song is an ode to human eros, it is also a Song that erects human eros as a signpost to something more. And so Klangwisan sets the poetry in a garden context which helps the reader of this volume to appropriate the significance of the Song in the wider panorama of the Hebrew Bible. And she does so by a creative deployment of the rabbinic concept of *pardes* in interpretation.

The comments immediately above were occasioned by the word "cosmic" in the title, an adjective which begs the question: "cosmic" what? And the answer is the "queen." This too is an important pointer to what goes on in this book, for it is a hint at Klangwisan's punt that the authorship of the Song is feminine and that the hero of the story is the beloved, sometimes referred to by her as "the Shulamith." Not all Songs scholarship will be convinced by this, but in the hands of Klangwisan the assumption works well. It also indicates that her literary approach is a consciously feminine one, not only because she is a woman but also because she believes that this is the best way to encounter the Song on its own terms. This does not mean that there is no analysis or proposition; the centre of the book is after all a discourse *analysis*. But it does mean that she seeks at every turn—and in fact has continued to do so even more intentionally in other writings since this was first penned—to allow the Song as much as is possible to speak in its own terms and not in those imposed by the interpreter.

Theological scholarship, including biblical scholarship, by its nature always works in "divers manners" with various intellectual partners, be they philosophy or literary criticism or sociology or anthropology—and the list could go on. While a number of reasons could be given for this being the case I would like to suggest two. First, in an encounter with an ancient text there are a number of gaps in our knowledge. In the face of this, there is a constant need to deploy intellectual tools the better to understand a text and a world that is unimaginably different from our own. Secondly, the Song, like any great piece of art, as we have noted, draws the reader towards the world beyond the text itself. As a function of the fact that the Song of Songs resides within the canon of Scripture, there is an inbuilt expectation on the part of many readers that the text in some way continues to speak into a contemporary context. For some this entails the expectation that the voice of God may in some way be discerned; for others it is a more general notion that a great and culture-forming ancient text might continue to beckon readers into her life. Either way, the engaged reader allows the text to lead him or her into a wider reality.

All sorts of intellectual tools may be deployed in this on-going quest, including with respect to the Song of Songs. One that has gained currency gathers around the notion of hermeneutical horizons, with its suggestion that an encounter with the ancient text entails the meeting of horizons. Much has been written about how this may be so, but one line of enquiry is to think in terms of language and communication and in particular to utilise the insights of pragmatic linguistics. The biblical text has a voice, and those who read enter into a responsive conversation with that voice. This calls forth an ethic of respect for the intentionality of the text, as well as a requirement that the reader responds in some way to that voice. A great deal of linguistic effort has gone into exploring how that actually might work as an encounter with an ancient text, and even more into how it might illuminate the encounter with an ancient text assumed by many to be sacred. Much of this effort gathers around the concept of "locution" as developed in Speech Act Theory. Locution is a useful concept because it pays attention both to the functional intent of an utterance or communication and to the outcome in those to whom the utterance is directed. In that respect it is a natural companion to the hermeneutical enterprise, which seeks to hear the voice of Scripture in contemporary context in a way that respects what that voice may have been trying to articulate in its ancient context. It thereby not only brokers the encounter of reader with text but also embarks on a journey towards a meeting of the contextual horizons of each.

One aspect of this linguistic and contextual encounter that is arguably under-explored by Speech Act Theory is the operation of inference in a communicative encounter. And that is addressed by the proponents of Relevance Theory, and further by those who seek to deploy it to understand the communicative potential of sacred texts. Klangwisan now joins the ranks of those deploying Relevance Theory in biblical studies, as she enables for her readers an encounter between contemporary reading and the ancient world and words and life of the Singer herself. In so doing she draws us, in the rabbinic terms laid out early in this book, below the surface or *peshat* of the text to the subterranean echoes, the *remez*. Or, to reprise a metaphor used earlier, she draws us into the Song itself and in doing so introduces us to the life of the Lover and the Beloved—and perhaps thereby opens the curtain a little to allow a glimpse of the very life of God. In doing so Klangwisan demonstrates both an impressive technical excellence, as evidenced in the discourse analysis on which her reading is based, and a rich affective and affectionate response to the poem and the lives it portrays. Because of that it is an honor for me to introduce this book.

Tim Meadowcroft
Laidlaw College, Auckland
October 2013

Preface

This book, *Earthing the Cosmic Queen*, explores the connection of poet, world and text in the Song of Songs, but as I reflect on the frame in which this work took place, I feel I must preface it. It was the beginning of a very long journey into the Song of Songs, "there and back again" when I began.

The journey of this study of this particular biblical book, the Song of Songs, took seven years. It seems fitting that I worked for this scroll the same amount of time it took Jacob to work for his beloved. I had spent a number of years prior learning about language, language theory and literature. I decided to embark upon a literary project on "something" from the Old Testament. So much of it drew me, the strange and fascinating journeys of the patriarchs, and the existential angst of the prophets, the annals of the Kings both good and bad. I held a deep belief that reading is transformative, and I felt that whichever book of the Old Testament I chose to embrace, it would change me forever, radically, if I let it, and I had firmly contracted to open myself up completely. For me, the choice came down to two books: the grief, poignancy and abject horror of the poetic Lamentations, or the raw poetic passions of the Song of Songs. Pleasure rather than pain won on the day and I set out to discover the lost hermeneutical key of a biblical love song.

I began the work a modernist, believing truly that the meaning of the Song of Songs was discoverable with modern language theory. I ended the work a postmodernist and deeply, profoundly humbled, transformed and enriched by an unconquerable poetry that loops, circles and flies.

I imagined the work would take several clever steps. The acronym constructed from *pardes* (Song 4:13) would structure these. Relevance Theory would fill them. And this is certainly the way the work initially progressed.

Preface

1. Read the text as it stands: *Peshat*
2. Trace the cues and echoes: *Remez*
3. Read the text in context: *Derasha*
4. Find the secret: *Sohd*

This is certainly how it all began. Little did I know it would take seven years to find the secret was not at all to be what I had thought. The novel, *The Alchemist*, by Paulo Coelho became profoundly evocative when I reread it during this time. A boy wanders across the top of Africa looking for the answer to the greatest question, that of "personal legend" or, that of the meaning of life, and finally finds that the answer was in the journey itself. Or, the jolt that accompanies sudden insight that came when reading the beautiful poetry of Constantine Cavafy, at the line where he writes: *And if you find her poor, / Ithaca did not deceive you. / As wise as you'll have become, with so much experience, / you'll have understood, by then, what these Ithacas mean.* The Song of Songs was to be my Ithaca: unconquerable, unassailable, and irrepressible. She was to be all these things. My blind determination, set to dissect the Song of Songs, was to be thoroughly foundered. In effect the opposite occurred. I was to be conquered and assailed by the very text I was trying to set in concrete, and looking back I wouldn't have it any other way.

The intellectual work around the Song of Songs was critical. The reading of the many skilled biblical scholars on the Song of Songs was necessary ground work and paved my way. But, the biblical scholar is after the Holy Grail, as I was, to find what it really, really means. Relevance Theory was to provide crucial colors and highlights that did surely lead to the deeps and abysses of the poetry. But Relevance Theory was finally only to light more clearly how deep and how endless the abysses were. It took a further work to describe this phenomenon, *Jouissance: A Cixousian Encounter with the Song of Songs* which I wrote following this work. It would take a whole ream of continental philosophers to facilitate for me a fitting articulation of the boundless limits of this text.

Yael Cameron Klangwisan
Rotorua, New Zealand
30 October 2013

Acknowledgments

There are many people to recognize, particularly the Laidlaw College community, which has been a nest of learning and a generous space for scholarship. I recall my colleagues and teachers who took interest in this work as it was taking shape and evolving, and I particularly recall those corridor epiphanies and inspirational lectures, off the cuff encouragements, and scintillating conversations with people as much in love with the biblical text as me: Tim Meadowcroft who has mentored me through all these years of study and the works that followed, but also my colleagues Nicola Hoggard Creegan, Phil Church, Mark Keown, John Hitchens, Stuart Lange, Jacqui Lloyd, and my fellow postgraduate travellers in the Hebrew Bible, Miriam Bier and Angeline Song. But there is a more intimate circle that I must distinguish: my parents who were grandparents and more over the past seven years, Yocheved and Betzelel; Avichai, who earthed the work for me into the reality rather than the imaginary of love; and my beautiful children, Shevarin and Shmu'el, who are to me, love incarnate.

Introduction

ברח דודי
ודמה-לך לצבי או לעפר האילים
על הרי בשמים¹

Flee my lover
And resemble a gazelle or young stag
Upon mountains of balsam²
(Song 8:14)

The scroll of the Song of Songs is a beautiful discourse, integrating narrative and prose; conjuring a context of music and dance. The scroll is a Pandora's Box of more than just lovers' ramblings. When encountered, face to face, it is complex, layered with meaning and subtle provocation, always threatening to tip the scales.

The Song of Songs came to be in a three-dimensional matrix: a certain poet or poets, at a certain time and in a certain (socio-geographic) space. This text, even if it seems these days to be a textual foundling, once had a "mother," that is, the one or ones who created the text and gave the poetry expression. This poet or poets lived and died at a distinct locus in the development of a culture. They lived within or against a predominant worldview. As such these texts are profoundly connected to the earth, that is, a certain time and discursive space, a certain geographical, political, social, and gendered context. Texts are the natural products of an author in that author's world.

1. The Hebrew text of the Song of Songs is sourced from the Masoretic Text of the Leningrad Codex as provided by the BHS. Elliger et al., *Biblia Hebraica Stuttgartensia*.

2. All English translations from the Song of Songs are my own using the Masoretic Text, unless otherwise noted.

Introduction

These texts however have a subsequent life that goes on after the death of the poet or author. They are freed from their cultural-cognitive unique space and reworked by subsequent redactors who are distant from the original context and inspiration. The text is disconnected from the mundane human existence from which it was given expression and through the annals of time original authorship is forgotten or misplaced. The text orphaned from its origins becomes mythic, particularly in sacred literature, as if it never had been human at all. The text itself becomes figured as an immaculate conception. The scroll is fixed within a canon representing a selection of such extant texts that communities over time have honored as sacred. The scroll becomes cosmic. Within the canon, unique and diverse texts become homogenized or reinscribed, with this relocation in an evolving and slowly concretising context. Their meanings, detached from what was once "earth," become interpreted as transcendent and otherworldly. The earthy, distinctive voice of a text is usurped by new foci aligning them to certain religious paradigms rather than what may have been originally. In the case of the Song of Songs, she became a Cosmic Queen in Judaism and Christianity—representing Israel, the *Shekinah*, or the transcendent church.

Paul Ricoeur would have scholarship value the historic interpretations of the Song of Songs,[3] even though the allegorical reading endorsed by both rabbinic[4] and patristic traditions[5] is flawed. It is, however, because of this allegorical reading that by such a chance, the text survives today in a primaveral form. The Song's content while undeniably prurient was crafted with a rich use of metaphor that could hold multiple meanings including those supporting the prevailing views of the religious establishment over time. The text's journey to canonization was still fraught with danger. The Talmud reveals that the elders had to insist that the Song of Songs "renders hands unclean."[6] This is evidence of significant dispute over the interpretation and thus the place of this book in the Hebrew canon. While modern scholarship must look beyond the allegorical in order to effect a reconnection of the Song to its origins, it must be considered that, at the very least,

---

3. Ricoeur, "The Nuptial Metaphor," 26.
4. Scherman, *Tanach*.
5. Pope, *Song of Songs*, 112.
6. Longman, *Song of Songs*, 21.

Introduction

the allegorical reading was a black knight that preserved the text for this generation's audience to engage anew.[7]

There is another scenario that I explore throughout this study. This text that wears the clothes of a woman's song, expressing inspiration, beauty and genius in the manipulation of language, with subtle depths in its reflection on ideas, and cunning use of a genre that allows for a dangerous degree of polysemy, finds a dais upon which the significance of its reflections on the enduring tenets of human experience may still be encountered. The Song of Songs becomes part of a corpus of works that engages human life and ideas about God, and wrestles with the status quo. This text continues to live and continues to find relevance, so to speak, as an extension of the poet/poetess, and engages philosophies and theologies of life within the symphony of wisdom literature and the wider array of Biblical literature.[8] These same words spark new conversations in each subsequent generation of scholarship as scholars seek out that elusive true intent. Thus, in the history of the Song of Songs' interpretation, the search for meaning has moved from allegorical and cosmic-sacred readings to a modern emphasis on secular readings with greater emphasis on cues to context.[9] This does not mean that the Song of Songs cannot be interpreted as having scope to engage both the divine and the carnal in its text. It is a deeply human text but its poetic character can also welcome the divine. Echoes and cues signalling the sacred within the Song of Songs are ubiquitous, pervasive, complex and intricate in intent. This multi-dimensionality opens the text to many interpretations. The title of this work is *Earthing the Cosmic Queen*. In the pages of the text of the Song of Songs I find the human and the divine earthed in each other in a richly sustaining way.

The existence of the Song of Songs is thus the end of a process that is both the function of the original poet's work and a function of the history of interpretation. The irony is that a religious establishment that through a

---

7. We know that the Qumran scribes omitted large passages of the text and considering those parts removed were highly erotic we can perhaps imply their reading of the Song was earthy and the omission an act of censorship. Abegg et al., *The Dead Sea Scrolls Bible*, 612. This had a crucial impact on the degree of preservation of the text in this community. This is why gratitude may be appropriate for the allegorical readings of other traditions that supported protecting the entire scroll against censorship and abandonment. Personalities such as Rabbi Akiba were instrumental in this regard. Longman, *Song of Songs*, 20–21.

8. In the Jewish canon the Song of Songs was placed with Ecclesiastes and other writings attributed to Solomon signifying it as a part of this corpus.

9. Ricoeur, "The Nuptial Metaphor," 265.

Introduction

flawed reading saved the Song of Songs may have also preserved a text that challenges and critiques it. The Song could validly be read as a vital corrective to the destructive rigidity of religious establishment.

These twists and turns in the history of reception and interpretation have preserved the Song of Songs for new generations of readers willing to explore its provocative character. It comes to us in a time when readers may have greater freedom to engage the very questions that the text still invokes. It is a paradox that the Song interpreted and reinterpreted, translated and redacted, exegeted and analyzed continues to evade its scholars in terms of absolute meaning, but readers who are prepared to follow the voice in the text, sensitive to its cues, and follow wherever it may lead, might just discover a tree of life.

Relevance Theory

Relevance theory is a modern linguistic theory that aligns itself well to the hermeneutical process. Championed by Dan Sperber and Deirdre Wilson,[10] the theory arose first in the linguistic field of Pragmatics and has of late been applied to biblical hermeneutics. Relevance Theory describes the process of communication as one that is earthed in actual contexts. A communication event from the perspective of Relevance Theory is birthed from the communicator's engagement, on the basis of the communicator's unique and shared environments, with other contextual environments which produce conflict or resonance. Thus, discovering authorial meaning in written discourse that has long since passed, demands, in the mind of a reader, a recreation of the "crisis" that produced the communication event in the first place.

In this reading of the Song of Songs I engage the concept of Relevance Theory and experiment with it as a hermeneutical tool.

Pardes

Pardes refers to a rabbinic exegetical method which I am adapting here to structure this study. My goal overall, in the tradition of Ricoeur,[11] is to

---

10. Sperber and Wilson's seminal work on Relevance Theory was first published in 1986. I have used their second edition as a basis for study. Sperber and Wilson, *Relevance*.

11. Ricoeur, "The Nuptial Metaphor," 265.

integrate both these new and old fruits of hermeneutics in a new reading of the Song of Songs that earths itself in the text's context.

Pardes is a Persian loan word arising once in the Hebrew Bible, in the Song of Songs (4:13).

[12]שלחיך פרדס רמנים עם פרי מגדים כפרים עם-נרדים:

The heroine of the Song is compared to an "orchard" of pomegranates; the way in which *pardes* is usually translated in the Song. The Persian word is the etymological origin of the English word "paradise," having passed through not only Biblical Hebrew, but Greek and Latin as well. *Pardes*, since the Song, has also been a sobriquet in Jewish mysticism for "enlightenment."[13] For the medieval, ecstatic scholar *pardes* became a metaphor for the sacred Torah. The Torah was a paradise of fruit. Reading the Torah became a work of *pardes* also. Communities like that of Baḥya ben Asher of Sargossa (1291) conceived the reading of this sacred literature as a series of epiphanies that move into the subterranean layers of a text guided by the meaning of *pardes* as its anacronym PRDS. For the purposes of this study, the character of *pardes* as an exegetical method is adapted from that of the Zohar.[14]

In the Zohar,[15] the reading begins with what is apparent on the surface, *peshat*, but then moves deeper, appreciating the hints, echoes and cues within the text: *remez*. At the level of *derasha*, I conceive the reading as a gaze that expands to the text's orientation or relation to other texts (my conception of *derasha* is a slight development away from the traditional kabbalistic exegetical model). The final reading is *sodh*, which is the deepest epiphany.[16] *Sodh* is often conceived of as mystical truth or secret. *Pardes* is a conceptual framework for this book and is exercised with the tools of Relevance Theory. This study explores the first three of the *pardes* series: *peshat* and *remez-derasha*. *Sodh* is the subject of future work.[17]

---

12. *pardes rimonim*.

13. See also Landy, "The Song of Songs," 307.

14. See note 101 of Liebes, *Studies in the Zohar*, 176. *Pardes* is implicitly understood as the method for reading the Hebrew Bible in the Zohar.

15. Scholem, *On the Kabbalah and its Symbolism*, 57. Scholem associates his reading of *pardes* (four levels of meaning) to Moses de León (1250–1305), the probable author of the Zohar.

16. This hermeneutical journey is also described in Jewish mysticism as an ascent through the halls of heaven.

17. Klangwisan, *Jouissance*.

Introduction

Chapter 1, *Pardes*, introduces Relevance Theory as a vibrant new fruit for the study of the Song. In the second chapter, with *Peshat*, the first level of *pardes*, the Song of Songs is analyzed as a unique text with Relevance Theory to explore the surface shape of the text. In the third chapter, *Remez*, the second level of *pardes*, the Song of Songs is read, attuned to its echoes and cues (implicatures). These integrate with *derasha*, or as I figure *derasha*, a reading of the Song inside the contextual environment of the poet, one that is infused with the sacred mythology of the Hebrews: the Garden of Eden.

1

Pardes: A Framework

And the LORD God formed out of the earth all the wild beasts and all the birds of the sky, and brought them to the man to see what he would call them; and whatever the man called each living creature, that would be its name ... but for Adam no fitting helper was found (Gen 2:19–20).[1]

Human beings have a proclivity towards naming. This process of naming is an act of communication. Its tool is language. Often the naming of the world is the guarded domain of the powerful ones, the sons of gods, kings. According to the text of Genesis it wasn't this way in the beginning. Human language in the Hebrew Bible began humbly and was solitary. In the Gen 2:19–20, the narrator recalls the first human naming his world but this event only served to accentuate his great loneliness.

The purposeful and complex uses of language are vastly more characteristic of the Hebrew Bible than simple naming. There is also a precedent in the Hebrew Bible for those critiquing the religious-political establishments of their time to use language as a tool of subversion against (illegitimate) authority. Such texts are scattered through Hebrew histories and the books of the prophets. The clever and creative condemnation of the King attributed to the prophet Natan in 2 Samuel 12:3 is a case in point.[2]

---

1. All English translations of the Hebrew Bible (apart from the Song of Songs, which is my own translation or otherwise marked) are from the New Jewish Publication Society Translation, 1985.

2. "... but the poor man had only one little ewe lamb that he had bought. He tended it and it grew up together with him and his children: it used to share his morsel of bread,

Earthing the Cosmic Queen

A theory of language is a core presumption often overlooked when attempting to resolve the ancient voices in Scripture. The Song of Songs' history of interpretation is shaped by various theories of language. These theories of language influence various hermeneutical methodologies. This first chapter, *Pardes*, after the medieval kabbalistic hermeneutic, will provide a rationale for the theory of language that I am engaging to read the Song of Songs. This chapter traces the development of language theory from the Greco-Roman view of language as a universal system, to more pragmatic theories of language that recognise the essential role of person and place. I also engage the ways in which these changing theories of language impact the reading of the Song.

Old Fruits to New

Aristotle, Augustine, and the Greco-Romans

Linguists have searched for a model that describes the true nature of language over many centuries.[3] Since Aristotle, ancient western scholarship labored in grammatical concerns. The Greeks and Romans perceived language as structural.[4] In the history of hermeneutics Augustine was a key figure who embraced the structural approach and elevated it in status to a universal theory of signs governed by laws (semiotics). He believed this semiotic system lay under all discoveries of meaning within the cuneiform symbols of those arcane and sacred manuscripts of the Bible. But more than this, the system was a milieu into which non-verbal communication, such

---

drink from his cup, and nestle in his bosom; it was like a daughter to him." This kind of creative critique of political power is ubiquitous in the stories and legends of the prophets, with marked examples being Amos, the legend of Micaiah, and the annals of Elisha and Elijah. It could be argued that it is an implied undercurrent in the Song of Songs as well.

3. The first recorded linguistic study is from Indian antiquity and was an eight-volume grammatical study of the great Sanskrit language. *Pánini*'s tome *Astadhyāyī* is dated as early as 600 BCE predating any Greek or Roman works. What followed was an exceptional tradition in Indian linguistic scholarship. Crystal, *Encyclopedia of Language*, 409.

4. Sperber and Wilson, *Relevance*. Before the time of the Greeks and Romans, the Indian linguists had progressed in their study of Sanskrit to even consider the semantics of language. Bharirhari 1,000 years later made the very important observation in the fifth century that a sentence consists of a flash of meaning—or in other words, he observed the importance of context in determining meaning. Coward and Raja, *The Philosophies of the Grammarians*, 81.

as religious ritual and cultural expressions, was structured as well.[5] The universities of Europe inherited this model[6] and the structural approach to language retained its dominance for more than a thousand years, even though "no semiotic law of any significance was ever discovered."[7]

The structural approach views language as obeying fundamental rules and it is the role of the structuralist to discover more clearly these rules in order to describe, predict and control language and thereby safe-guard the derivation of meaning. The structural approach conceives that grammar and vocabulary together (a knowledge base) are the fundamentals of language and thus communication. The structuralist approach centres on the coding-decoding process in verbal communication, with the word being the basic unit of meaning.[8] At the cognitive level a writer transforms thought-messages to verbal code (text). A reader on recognising and decoding the text then reproduces and comprehends the thought-messages.[9] The knowledge of language via this code model allows us to analyze the grammatical role of each word in a phrase, which is no doubt a very good place to start in exegesis of a foreign and ancient text. However, this sort of analysis gives no firm place to the reality of the communication event as situated within a social/cultural/circumstantial locus. In spite of great advances in semiotics such as Chomsky's transformational grammar, language, as Sperber deftly puts it, is *sui generis*.[10]

The code model provides us with the following of the Song 1:1: a noun, masculine, singular, construct: *[the] song*, then, noun, masculine, plural, with definite article, *of songs*, followed by a relative clause (relative pronoun, preposition, and proper name): *which is of/to Shlomo*.

שיר השירים אשר לשלמה

---

5. Sperber and Wilson, *Relevance*, 6.

6. Crystal, *Cambridge Encyclopedia of Language*, 3.

7. Sperber and Wilson, *Relevance*, 7. Of course there is also clear opposition against the movements of modern and post-modern linguistics into biblical hermeneutics. Scholars such as Robert Thomas see modern linguistics as having an ambiguous, uncertain and fatally subjective view of language to which the solid structure of the semiotic view is far preferable. Thomas, "Modern Linguistics Versus Traditional Hermeneutics," 42.

8. Thiselton, "Semantics," 76.

9. Sperber and Wilson, *Relevance*, 4.

10. Ibid., 8.

This text is atomised into smaller and smaller units so that hermeneutics may be carried out comprehensively word for word. This routine exegesis overlooks modern insights that suggest that a text requires enlarging through the context-sensitive embedding of *chunks of language*.[11] The traditional approach cannot answer questions about Song 1:1 such as "What did the poet intend through this comment?" and "What did the original audience appreciate by this statement and why?" Song 1:1 at the *peshat* level makes a clear link between the scroll of the Song and *Shlomo*. This either attributes the Song as the handiwork of *Shlomo* or seeks to set the Song of Songs in the corpus of literature of which *Shlomo* was considered a patron.[12] At the level of *remez* the cue might be in the consonants of the name. It may represent a riddle, such as Hebrew poets are wont to employ. Rashi famously posited that *Shlomo* should be read as an acronym like *pardes*, so that *Shlomo* is read as *the One to whom peace belongs*.[13]

Saussure and Chomsky

Until Ferdinand de Saussure, western language theory consisted of empirical, structural studies of the linguistic code system. However while grammars and concordances play important roles in linguistic study they do not deal with the essentially pragmatic nature of language and its crucial significance for making meaning. Published in his seminal *Cours du linguistique générale*, 1916, Saussure's gift to the development of linguistic theory was not in particular his enduring belief that language is a system of signs (semiotics), but his observation that communication consists of *Langue et Parole*.[14] This significant observation deeply influenced the future development of linguistic theory by marking the discrepancy between the knowledge about a code system (semiotics) and actual communication. Pragmatic and subjective content is ultimately significant, as Noam Chomsky similarly realised when he, like Saussure, developed a linguistic theory that attached knowledge of linguistic codes, which he called *competence*, to the use of language in real situations, *performance*.[15] It was Chomsky's observations of language in action that founded Modern Linguistics. The

---

11. Thiselton, "Semantics," 78.
12. Keel draws a similar conclusion in *The Song of Songs*, 39.
13. Scherman, ed., *Tanach*, 1682 (note 1:1).
14. Saussure, *Course in General Linguistics*, 77.
15. Chomsky, *Language and Mind*, 4, 23ff.

practical and shared aspects of language as *communication* were clearly of a higher significance for making meaning than the physical code components themselves. In the communication event each linguistic unit finds value only "in relationship to the whole."[16] And that *whole* can never be detached from the event that produced it.

Language as a universal grammatical system has been the base presumption for traditional and conventional biblical hermeneutics for the Western world since the Greco-Roman era.[17] Sperber and Wilson represent the Modern Linguistics corpus when they label the structural approach "descriptively inadequate."[18] The process of communication is more complex than semiotic theory's core assumption of the coding-decoding model and conversely, conflations of structural, semiotic theories in order to make sense of language's exceptionalities make them so complex they cease to function. *Ce qui est trop simple est faux, ce qui est trop complexe est inutilisable.*[19] Particularly when cognitive processes are incorporated, *code* is better seen as an important tool in the communication event rather than a model for it:

> Comprehension involves more than the decoding of a linguistic signal. Although a language can be seen as a code which pairs phonetic and semantic representations, much recent work . . . shows that there is a gap between the semantic representations of sentences and the thoughts actually communicated by utterances.[20]

The code model does not adequately describe a whole gamut of actual communication phenomena concerned with time and space, person and place. Earthed by the reality of the moment (the crisis) catalysing the communication event, humans are able to clarify each other's utterances using signs not necessarily sourced from the abstract realm of linguistic knowledge. For example, with, *Seize the little jackals! / Vine-spoilers!! / When our vineyards bud* (2:15), the prose is not interpretable via the structuralist's

---

16. Saussure, *Course in General Linguistics*, 114.

17. Thomas, "Modern Linguistics Versus Traditional Hermeneutics," 23, describes the Grammatic-historical tradition of hermeneutics as "long-held"; Crystal, *Encyclopedia of Language*, 408–11, describes the line of Greco-Roman thought through to twentieth-century Western paradigms regarding linguistic study. See also Thiselton, "Semantics."

18. Sperber and Wilson, "Précis of Relevance," 697.

19. A French maxim: what is too simple is wrong and what is too complex can't be used.

20. Sperber and Wilson, "Précis of Relevance," 697.

code model because it requires contextual input in order to produce the identity of the speakers and referents, their context and therefore the meaning. In Israel at the time, jackals did have a habit of gnawing on the newly budded vines.[21] Catching jackals before they destroyed the fragile vines was a common activity for many a Hebrew vintner. Vineyards were commonly attached to the home. However in the Song, the image *vineyard* is also metaphorical. In the preceding lines of the Song the poet has begun to subtly connect the image of "vineyard" to the image of the young woman, and in particular, her sexuality. In the context, the "jackals" are by implication those young men who are attracted to the young woman, her sexuality, and are thus treated as threats by the heroine's male relatives who may be speaking here. With this interpretation gained from the sociolinguistic aspects of language and context, it is clear that structural approaches to biblical interpretation require the support of linguistic theories that can assist the reconnection of the language of the Song of Songs to the moment that produced it.

Human beings naturally communicate via semantically incomplete sentences. In Song 1:2 the *Shulamith*[22] emphatically utters: *Let him kiss me with the kisses of his mouth!* The sentence only makes sense semantically when considered alongside its co-text, and the relevant contextual assumptions regarding the nature of such an emphatic statement. The semiotic model here cannot cope with the ambiguity of the utterance. Human beings are able to identify illocutionary force when they converse. Human communicators recognize the difference between ironic, sarcastic, fantastic and literal statements, and recover implicit import. None of these common communicative tasks are able to be represented in the semiotic model.[23]

---

21. Carey Ellen Walsh goes into detail regarding the vineyard imagery occurring in the Song. Walsh, *Exquisite Desire*, 129–32.

22. The author of the Song of Songs creates a personae of the female protagonist but does not name her. With respect to this purposed authorial ambiguity I call her *the Shulamith* or "the heroine." In the Song of Songs, the descriptor *Shulamith* only occurs twice in chapter 6. However the Song of Songs is a song deeply concerned with "shalom" or peace and several key words belonging to the root שלם abound in the Song including *Shulamith*. שלם is found in the name *Shlomo* which occurs ubiquitously in the Song and significantly 7 times, and to whom the Song is initially attributed. The thread that plays upon שלם may also be tied to Jerusalem (city of shalom) rhythmically refrained eight times in the Song of Songs.

23. Sperber and Wilson, "Précis of Relevance," 698.

The contextual environment is a key element disambiguating these circumstances.[24]

The semiotic model simply does not provide the necessary representations of significant phenomena in the communication process and because of its limitation to lexicology and grammar it cannot emphasise the role of reality/actuality in language creation and the prioritising of meaning. Without connection to reality, language is construed through grammar and words in ways not necessarily related to the events that originally catalyzed that language. David Clark writes on how this failure of the code model has been exploited in hermeneutics:

> They say that because language functions in complex ways according to the grammatical rules that govern what can and cannot be said in a particular form of life, language may not refer at all. This means they relate the words "truth" and "meaning," not to reality, but to grammar. Meaning is [to them] not a function of a connection of language to reality, but of language to more language.[25]

Anthony Thiselton makes the severe statement that traditional understanding of the nature of language is based on ignorance rather than logic and genuine advances in semantics were decisively inhibited by those same adherents.[26]

Wittgenstein and Russell

Ludwig Wittgenstein and Bertrand Russell are two influential philosophers supplementing the iconoclastic era in Linguistics. The propositions of Wittgenstein's *Tractatus Logico-Philosophicus* (1922) and Russell's Theory of Descriptions initially appearing in the essay "On Denoting" (1905) led to a rethinking of human cognition and communication. Comprehension is not as simple as decoding. Russell's contribution is the recognition that even chunks of meaning-filled language are not nearly as important as the propositions behind them.[27] Knowledge of the grammar and vocabulary of

---

24. Gutt, *Relevance Theory*, 12.
25. Clark, *To Know and Love God*, 377.
26. Thiselton, "Semantics," 78.
27. Russel's thesis is often paraphrased as "the apparent logical form of a proposition need not be the real on" (Russell, "On Denoting," 479–93).

a sentence does not necessarily provide a predictable interpretation of the proposition behind it. Regarding biblical texts, Croatto suggests:

> A text is something structured and finished. It has limits and internal relationships. . . . The original sender disappears in a text . . . Nor is the first receiver or interlocutor present . . . For the same reason the horizon of the original discourse disappears; the cultural and historical context is no longer the same; current addressees receiving the message have another "world" of interests, concerns, culture and so on.[28]

In ancient texts there is a loss of context and the all-important propositions behind the text become increasingly inaccessible to the modern reader. Without a sure understanding of these propositions, the text becomes more and more at risk of the threats of either impotency or abuse. Thiselton points out that for biblical interpretation a reconstruction of this extra-linguistic situation is necessary on purely linguistic grounds.[29] Therefore, from the perspective of modern language theory, *eisegesis*, or a careful "reading in" of context sensitive information must have a defined place in the hermeneutical endeavour.[30]

Discourse

As part of language theory's redefinition (as *communication events*), language theorists began to study the place of *discourse* in language. Communication is a multi-part process entailing the roles, responsibilities and actions of author and addressee further set into a particular environmental milieu. Discourse itself was found to be a complex phenomenon that could involve the written and spoken word as well as non-verbal communication such as silence. What discourse researchers found was that sequence and relationship of language chunks and *utterances* were as important as

---

28. Croatto, *Theory of Reading*, 16.
29. Thiselton, "Semantics," 79.
30. See also Croatto, *Theory of Reading*, 66–76. By *eisegesis*, I mean that the construction of meaning from ancient texts must be a process of "reading in" the relevant contextual and cognitive environments. Croatto explores the notion of *eisegesis* as critical to biblical hermeneutics throughout his book particularly chapter 3. It is inevitable with the degree of displacement of the modern audience that a (narrow) range of polysemy will continue to exist in the interpretation of biblical texts. This semantic corridor (rather than fixed locus of a closed interpretation) is healthy for biblical scholarship and theology and not detrimental as Thomas, "Modern Linguistics" would suggest.

Pardes: A Framework

the code itself because they provide coherence and cues to meaning.[31] So while intricate, due to diverse internal and external variables, the idea of discourse does have significance for literary analysis.

In the Song of Songs, this complex connection of utterances is a case in point. While appearing discontinuous at the *peshat* level, the text finds coherence in the relationships between threads of discourse that flow between seemingly discontinuous sections.[32] The Song exhibits multiple interweaving threads of discourse. One tendril of discourse concerns *rest*. A discourse about the concept of *rest* (and associated imagery i.e., *bed* or *recline*) appears as an interior monologue that surfaces intermittently in the text. It is circular rather than linear and journeys through a variety of intersecting paradigms. The key linking feature is the strategic use of pronouns (you, he, ours, mine) which create in the reader a mood of distance or closeness to the protagonist. The figure that follows bears this out.

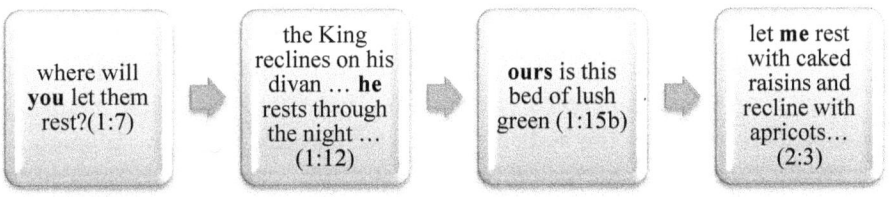

Figure 1: The initial discourse thread around the imagery of "rest."

The linguistic field of Pragmatics in which the study of Discourse finds itself, takes into account the role of settings, conventions, moods and audience as well as a range of other factors, embracing the inherent subjectivity and *sui generis* nature of human communication. It overlaps into all the other approaches to language and in effect links them together: sociolinguistics, stylistics, semantics, grammar and psycholinguistics. Speech Act Theory[33] and Relevance Theory were developments in Prag-

---

31. The same conclusion drawn by the Indian linguist "Bhartṛhari" over a thousand years prior (500 CE). Coward and Raja, *The Philosophies*, 81.

32. On the notion of cleaving and joining within the Song's structure Landy writes persuasively, "the poem is integrated as the lovers are integrated . . . Yet there is also an element of disunity in the Song, in the violence with which it dismembers the body . . ." (Landy, "The Song of Songs," 315–16).

33. Vanhoozer sees Speech Act Theory as one of the more significant linguistc developments with respect to philosophy and theology. Vanhoozer, "From Speech Acts to Scripture Acts," 3.

matics in response to the increasing recognition of the non-structural nature of real communication. Speech Act Theory is a process of convention where speech acts are recognised as active and categorised according to their action. Relevance Theory, on another tangent, describes the particular relationship between inference and cognition in communication.

Speech Acts

The key to meaning via recognition of *speech acts* is in the intent of the communicator and the impact on the audience. The question becomes: "What are the intentions of the speaker or writer?" or significantly "What are the effects of this *utterance* on the audience?" J. L. Austin, the father of modern Speech Act Theory, challenged the perceived passive function of communication, by recognizing its very active components.[34] For example language enables humans to carry out a wide range of actions: to believe, challenge, promise, apologize or declare.[35] Speaking and writing are communicative acts. Every act of communication is loaded with intention.[36] Intentions may range from warning people of impending danger to encouraging a crowd with stirring words. The audience is affected by each communication and responds in some way. They may take heed and escape danger. They may be encouraged and inspired.[37] In some situations an audience may ignore a communication. Perhaps the speaker or writer lacked authority, or ability, or may have been insincere.[38]

---

34. Constatives are descriptive utterances or assertions that can be judged as true or false. They have no performative quality. Performatives pervade language and perform acts or create states of affairs i.e., "I do" in the marriage ceremony. Austin, *How to Do Things with Words*, 1–11.

35. Each of these speech acts represent Searle's illocutionary acts: representatives, directives, commissives, expressives and declarations. Searle, *Expression and Meaning*, 1–29. See also Searle, *Intentionality*, 166.

36. Austin calls the act of saying something (producing language) without respect to its content, "locutionary." This is really the domain of the structuralist approach to knowledge. Vanhoozer, "From Speech Acts," 15. Austin describes the "illocutionary" force as the recognition of intent in language—an illocutionary speech act may warn, encourage, show love to the addressee. It may also be in the form of a question where an answer is expected. Austin, *How to Do Things with Words*, 94, 98.

37. The "perlocutionary act": to be warned, to be encouraged, to be loved, is the response to the locutionary act (saying or writing something) of the addressee. Ibid., 99.

38. For the communicative intent to be successful Austin recognized "felicity conditions" must be met according to social convention. For example some utterances require

Pardes: A Framework

In chapter 1 of the Song of Songs, the categories of speech acts can be seen in the discourse of the players. The *Shulamith*'s hero utters a declaration: *So beautiful, my friend / So beautiful / Your eyes are doves* (1:15).

This direct speech in Speech Act terminology is called a *locutionary act*, but the *illocutionary force* of this speech—the intent of the Lover—was informing and declarative, to express his perspective of his beloved, in such a way that she would want to respond to him. Thus the *perlocutionary* force (the effect on the addressee) was such a response. Her response is commissive,[39] her want is clear. However, her speech takes the generic form of a declaration. We understand her intent by looking through the words to the proposition behind them. We recognize her intention in that she shares his desire and yearns to reciprocate:—*You are beautiful, my beloved / So gentle!* (1:16).

The *commissive* force is implicit. She is contracting, vowing, promising with a simple declaration. The underlying intent is almost tangible in its strength.

Inference

Grice could be credited with discovering the basis upon which Speech Act Theory and Relevance Theory rest. He saw that the nature of language, of communication was primarily the expression and recognition of intentions. He also recognized that "utterances raise expectations of relevance," and importantly that communication creates conditions for its own success.[40] Or, as Sperber and Wilson describe the phenomenon, "The very act of communicating creates expectations, which it then exploits."[41]

In 1986, Dan Sperber and Dierdre Wilson advanced the theory by analyzing the role of cognition in an inferential model of communication. The crucial consideration for these scholars was meaning and how humans

---

the speaker to have authority or credibility, other categories of utterance require the speaker to be sincere (i.e., apologizing), while other categories like sarcasm or irony may mean the speaker or author is purposefully insincere. Where the audience or author is unaware of convention the communication will fail. Ibid., 12–24.

39. The commissive is the intention of the speaker to commit to bringing about a certain course of action. Searle, *Expression and Meaning*, 8.

40. On the whole subject of utterances and intention see, Grice, *Studies in the Way of Words*, 86–116; Wilson and Sperber, "Relevance Theory," 607. See also, Pattemore, *The People of God in the Apocalypse*, 14.

41. Sperber and Wilson, "Précis of Relevance," 699.

arrive at meaning through their utterances. In an inferential process one takes "a set of premises as input and yields as output a set of conclusions which follow logically from . . . the premises."[42] It is not a simple code-decode process. Comprehension is best understood as an inferential process. Grice studied the propensity of human communication to be indirect, with remarkable reliance on assumptions within discourse.

> My lover descended into his garden
> Through terraces of balsam
> To shepherd in the gardens
> And harvest the lotus (Song 6:2)

In reading the Song of Songs we must make many assumptions. This verse in particular requires inference for every *stich*. The garden is assumed as a metaphor for the heroine. The terraces of balsam are aspects of the heroine that attract her lover, i.e., her scent, her inner qualities, her body. The inference of *shepherding* in the gardens (2:16; 6:2, 3) is the initial stages of love-making and quite confidently one might assume *harvesting the lotus* (6:2) is the meat of sexual union. But a poet would rarely write in such bald terms. Inference enables exploration of a delicate subject. Erotic literature (and art) uses the inferential process in cognition particularly because it requires the reader to create erotic meaning from carefully selected, non-explicit imagery.[43]

Once again, the interpretation of such discourse, so evident in the Song of Songs involves understanding linguistic and situational contexts and embedding these in the reading. These contexts act as a matrix within which such language chunks, pregnant with meaning, can be oriented. It is the language fixed in its correct circumstantial matrix that provides cues to the appropriate inference.

Relevance Theory

A holistic theory of language must also take into account the presuppositions of communicators, both author and audience and this is where Relevance Theory progressed beyond Speech Act Theory. In the following

---

42. Ibid., 698.

43. Walsh discusses the significance of inference in erotic literature eloquently in Walsh, *Exquisite Desire*, 41–45.

Pardes: A Framework

example from the Song of Songs the author exploits the presuppositions of the audience in a startling way:

> Promise me [*hishbati*], daughters of Jerusalem
> By the gazelles [*zva'ot*]
> By the deer [*ayelot*] in the field [*sadeh*]
> That you will never rouse nor awaken love
> Until it is full (Song 2:7; 3:5)

André LaCocque is convinced on a sociolinguistic basis that in the context of the ancient Near East, this formulaic utterance would presuppose a vow to a god, however, in the Song of Songs the oath is made to field creatures.[44] The audience of this text would be perplexed at the possible irreverence of this apparently purposeful "cross-purpose" in the text. The reader is persuaded to look more closely. At the level of morphology and etymology the names of the creatures to which the oath is made—*zva'ot, ayelot, sadeh*—have an uncanny proximity to—*sebaot, eloah, shaddai*—three titles associated with YHWH.[45] If so, the mood in the Song becomes one of movement from distance to imminence, a common phenomenon in the Song that will be explored in *Peshat*. The God-of-armies is brought disturbingly close to earth through artistic sleight of hand.[46]

From this one example it can be seen how assumptions and implications play critical roles in discourse and therefore need to be reflected in a theory of language. So while Speech Act Theory deals with the force behind words spoken, Relevance Theory takes into account the role of assumptions and implications (inferences) behind the words uttered. Relevance Theory situates comprehension in the cognitive realm, and the interaction of the cognitive realm with actuality. The nature of language as a negotiation or tension between cognition and the physical and social environment is a crucial element in establishing the meaning that a text had for a particular audience.

---

44. See also LaCocque, "The Shulamite," 254–55.
45. Ibid., 255.
46. Scott sees this allusion to crossing forbidden boundaries as a quality of erotic-sacred literature that seeks to symbolize *mystery*, the mystery of sexuality. Scott, "Radha in the Erotic Play of the Universe," 239–42.

Cognitive Environment and Mutual Manifestness

What Sperber and Wilson mean by cognitive environment[47] is not simply the external environment that surrounds a person, nor even the broader "discursive space of a culture,"[48] but of all the facts that a person has access to, both external and internal.

Internal facts are those stored from life experience, formal learning and social learning. They consist of whatever is in the memory, to what is apparent immediately through the senses and whatever one is capable of becoming aware of by representation. This cognitive environment not only embodies facts but also a vast array of more abstract conceptions: *assumptions*.

Mutual manifestness is also an important concept in the Relevance theoretic scheme of the process of communication. In Relevance Theory each human has a unique cognitive environment; however, at many points the cognitive environments of individuals overlap. For example, in the scroll of the Song of Songs, the hero and heroine overlap in their cognitive environments in their experience of what it is to be lovers in their social world. However the heroine sees their world from her perspective and her hero sees their world from his, thus there are areas in which even the lovers' cognitive environments do not overlap and these differences collide, as in this beautiful series of couplets:

> I am a crocus of the Sharon plain
> A valley-lotus
> —As a lotus among brambles
> So is my love
> Among young women (Song 2:1–2)

The lovers in the Song both understand what it is to be human, to live in their culture, and the intrinsic reward of being passionately in love and loved in return. The heroine and her hero do not share the same facts regarding her inherent value. The heroine describes herself as a common field flower thriving only by his love. He contests her self-knowledge with his response. He claims that she is more beautiful than any other. Her

---

47. "A cognitive environment of an individual is a set of facts that are manifest to him. A fact is manifest to the individual at a given time if, and only if, the individual is capable at the time of representing it mentally and accepting its representation as true or probably true" (Sperber and Wilson, "Précis of Relevance," 699).

48. Culler, *The Pursuit of Signs*, 103.

self-claims might be seen to grow in confidence from this point in the Song. The hero does not share tangibly the cognitive environment that the heroine, the *Shulamith*, shares with her young women friends. Only they can understand what it is to be an unmarried woman in that culture, women who in a patriarchal society have experienced vulnerability and danger of being alone near other men (i.e., Song 5:7): *They beat me / They bruised me / They tore at my veil.*

When human beings share a mutual cognitive environment it means that many of the facts and assumptions will be shared as well; dealt with in the same way cognitively. These shared assumptions and facts are termed *mutually manifest*. When the two lovers revel in their secret garden, their frantic, whispered discourse marks the boundaries of their shared cognitive environments. Yet the heroine also complains that they cannot share enough. The lovers still have non-mutual cognitive environments: *I would lead you and bring you to my mother's house . . .* (8:1). There is an insurmountable gap between them.

Ostensive-Inferential Communication

New information, such as the hero's differing perspective on the *Shulamith's* beauty, affects the other's cognitive environment. This phenomenon identified by Relevance Theory highlights difference but can also catalyze and transform the other's sense of the world. The cognitive environments of communicators are in continual change as new information becomes manifest to them: through knowledge, through observation, through life experience. These new facts confirm assumptions already held or may catalyze transformation in the cognitive environment, perhaps causing one to throw out an old assumption and take on a new one. When contradicted by her hero, the heroine reforms her self-image on the basis of what was made manifest to her: *I am a wall, and my breasts are like towers/ so in his view I am like one who finds shalom* (8:10). The heroine's cognitive environment might indeed have changed significantly through her lover's communication. By chapter 8 she is claiming her inherent value without the slightest shade of self-denigration. She was formerly a simple field flower. Now she rules herself.

When someone communicates, that person is innately seeking to create change in the other's cognitive environment. In Relevance Theory, this inclination is called the *informative intention*. In human communication, verbal or non-verbal, participants in discourse communicate on the basis of what they might understand as the shared or mutual cognitive environment, but with the intention of presenting new information that comes from difference. These communications to others can be strong or weak, i.e., communications that are explicit or implicit. A communicator can also communicate information unintentionally.

Degrees of Relevance—Optimality

What one communicates to another consists of symbols, both verbal and non-verbal, acting as guides and signposts, after taking into account what items the other will need and expect in order to understand. Relevance Theory therefore illuminates the intricacies of human cognition, that is, the way humans process and discover input. Input surrounds us. If one tried to process all the input that is manifest even in a momentary flash of time one would not be able to cope. Thus input only becomes relevant if it produces what Sperber and Wilson call *positive effects* in the mind of the addressee. This input has been flagged as relevant and is assimilated into that person's pre-existing cognitive environment, an environment full of knowledge.[49] When presented with input one processes it with respect to the knowledge he or she already has stored concerning it. Input with highest relevance (optimum relevance) will be prioritised by the reader or listener.[50]

In what we can make of the story of the lovers in the Song of Songs it is not hard to discern a scenario of passionate desire and consummation deferred. This scenario maintains relevance even centuries later. Romance and in particular romantic tragedy still hasn't grown old. Humans seem innately drawn to it.

> On my bed at night
> I yearned for him
> The one I love with all my breath (Song 3:1)

The reader is primed towards this input, most would find it optimally relevant, forming the realization that the heroine is in the throes of new love and frustrated at being separated from her hero. However the same language could fail to produce these obvious positive effects in the minds

---

49. Ibid. This knowledge is social, factual, cultural and entails ethics and values.

50. This is the cognitive principle of relevance. Human cognition tends to be geared to the maximization of relevance. Wilson and Sperber, "Relevance Theory," 610.

of some audiences because of the dominance of the frame in which this particular text is set, i.e., the canon of the Bible. The sheer distance in space and time between the birth of the Song and the current day is not the issue. At this point in the Song the meaning that is most relevant at the surface or *peshat* level is the enduring experience of the *human* condition and particularly the condition of sexual love. But, for many biblical scholars both Patristic and Rabbinic, that meaning (i.e., two teenaged lovers revelling in the erotic roller coaster of love) in the context of sacred scripture was unacceptable and incompatible. Complex allegorical interpretations concerning God and Israel or God and church (in Christian tradition) were devised to compensate.[51] There are many shades of meaning in the Song of Songs that elude the contemporary reader and these must have been strikingly obvious to those who lived in the poet's milieu but the broader meanings in this text and the text's subsequent relevance in the wider array of biblical literature continue to mean for challenging exegetical work.

The poet behind the Song of Songs depends heavily on the creation of cognitive representations. The poet's words form pictures/images that point to multiple meanings even beyond that of the immediate semantic range of the linguistic unit.[52] The natural world has symbolic meaning for poet's portrayal of the lovers' discourse and thus the reader.[53] Their garden riots with resins, fragrances, wild animals, domestic animals, flowers, fruits, trees and vines. All of it (perhaps apart from the jackals) is implicitly beneficial and benevolent. The information that the poet hopes will become pertinent to the reader, after processing the ostensive input of *creation* in the lovers' world, may be that the whole of nature celebrates and legitimizes the romance. These are the cognitive effects.

Perhaps the poet intends through her rhetoric to persuade her audience of the legitimacy of the heroine's *affaire de coeur*.[54] Whether the poet's

---

51. The English translation in the Tanach follows the Rabbinic (Rashi) allegorical interpretation of the Song. The allegorization of the Song was so complex, an entirely new song was written to compensate. See the "Song of Songs" in Scherman, *Tanach*.

52. Synesthesia is a poetic stylistic that comes into play in the Song and increases the degree of polysemy.

53. Phyllis Trible draws out this aspect of the Song of Songs concerning the lovers' relationship with animals in the Song. Trible, "Love's Lyrics Redeemed," 154–55.

54. This would then fall within the category of ostensive-inferential communication within Relevance Theory. The poet would have had an informative intention, which is the intention to inform an audience of something; a communicative intention. At an even more complex level the poet may have intended to inform the audience of her informative intention. Sperber and Wilson, *Relevance*, 61.

use of these symbols would be optimally relevant to disapproving male relatives (Song 1:6) is another matter. The poet imaged that the speech acts attributed to the Shulamith would have optimal relevance for her hero and ultimately the reader.[55] Input is thus verbal and non-verbal; symbolic or factual. In discourse participants often make a deduction from non-verbal input before confirming the point verbally. In poetry, where non-verbal input is evoked in the imagery arising from a text, a complex interplay occurs between the reader's ability to draw relevant assumptions and the author's ability to deftly predict and produce those assumptions in the reader. It is a beautiful dance in the Song of Songs.

In the Song of the *Shulamith* and her hero, reading the speech play between the two, it could be deduced that the work of the non-verbal input in the form of imagery cultivated by *Shulamith* is primed to draw the attention of the hero to her attributes: her body, her eyes, her movement. This attention is realised when in chapter 7:2–10 her hero drifts into soliloquy on this very subject.[56] The difference between non-verbal and verbal communication is that the linguistic code houses the logical forms that produce conceptual representations: thoughts. These thoughts provide input to the audience's inferential comprehension process and the audience comprehends. The difference is that the spoken or written word is capable of a higher degree of explicitness than non-verbal communication.

Explicatures, Implicatures, and Literature

When reading poetry, one is presented in literal terms, with a linguistic code. The code is fashioned into prose and from this prose, the reader must determine meaning. However from the perspective of Relevance Theory, the prose/code must be enriched contextually in several ways in order to yield the meaning that might represent the poet's intention. This requires an appropriate set of contextual assumptions, which the original

---

55. That is the "Communicative principle of relevance" which reads that "every ostensive stimulus conveys a presumption of its own relevance." In terms of *Shulamith's* speech, she would believe that what she was saying would make sense to the person she intended to say it to. Making sense is about "Optimal relevance." That is, an ostensive stimulus is optimally relevant to an audience if "it is relevant enough to be worth the audience's processing effort, OR it is the most relevant one compatible with communicator's abilities and preferences." The disapproving male relatives would not have preferences compatible to the two lovers and therefore do not understand. Ibid., 158.

56. Or perhaps a verbal conversation with her response non-verbal.

Pardes: A Framework

addressees/audiences must have also supplied. In the case of a reader made de facto by culture, time, and circumstance, that reader then must attempt to re-imagine the possible cognitive environments of the supposed original audience in order to access the poet's intent.

Naturally humans will follow a certain process of communication and Relevance Theory is a description of this interpersonal negotiation that occurs even with the written word. The communicative principle of relevance and the notion of optimal relevance define how a hypothesis is constructed about the poet's meaning by the reader or hearer. The primary audience most often will negotiate the linguistic code; and by following a path of least effort, enrich it contextually at the explicit level and complement it at the implicit level until the resulting interpretation meets particular expectations of relevance.[57] A writer generally formulates her writing so that the first interpretation to satisfy the intended audience's expectation of relevance is the one that she intended to convey. A piece of writing with two apparently satisfactory competing interpretations, would cause the audience unnecessary work in choosing between them. The resulting interpretation would be less than optimally relevant.[58]

The primary audience will anticipate, create and develop hypotheses against a background of expectations and also revise hypotheses or elaborate them as the text unfolds. The audience brings a presumption of relevance, but more specific expectations about how the utterance will be relevant personally. These will be proportional to the cognitive effects they are likely to achieve. So the whole process of comprehension involves a non-demonstrative inference process embedded within the overall process of constructing a hypothesis about the poet's meaning.[59]

In the history of interpretation of the Song we can see how various audiences through time have sought optimal relevance from the Song.

---

57. Relevance-theoretic comprehension procedure as explained by Wilson and Sperber, "Relevance Theory" is as follows: "A) Follow a path of least effort in computing cognitive effects: Test interpretive hypotheses (disambiguations, reference resolutions, implicatures, etc.) in order of accessibility. B) Stop when your expectations of relevance are satisfied" (Wilson and Sperber, "Relevance Theory," 629).

58. Stephen Pattemore explores this concept in Pattemore, *The People of God*, 17, 80. Also note in the allegorical tradition (as aforementioned) the danger of "lay-readers" drawing the wrong conclusion (no matter how relevant it seemed) meant that particularly in the Rabbinic tradition an entirely new song was written for translations into vernacular tongues. Scherman, *Tanach*. In the Rabbinic tradition embargoes were also placed on whom and at what age a person might read this "holy of holies."

59. Wilson and Sperber, "Relevance Theory," 630ff.

Traditional interpretations were based on an allegory of the love between God and Israel or God and the church. It is clear that these audiences presumed, due to the canonization of the Song, that spirituality must be the object. The heroine was obviously, with the evidence of prophetic imagery, Israel (or the church). The male protagonist was thus most logically, God. Items like the "two breasts" (Song 4:5; 7:3) became clearly symbolic of the Old and New Testament or Moses and Aaron in rabbinic tradition.[60] But the allegorical reading is flawed in its logic in chapter 7 where the mother travails and gives birth to "God," whom the heroine claims she awakens.[61] The poet must either be poorly skilled in the construction of allegory or this particular allegory is not what the poet imagined as her audience's reading. And it is what the poet had in mind that is of vital interest.

Poetry, Style, and Metaphor

Relevance Theory can be used to explain stylistic qualities in literature, the choice of which are guided by the assessment of her audience by the poet for mutual understanding. An utterance containing poetic effects will encourage a reader to explore and process further what the implications are, with certain expectations of being rewarded with meaning. Highly poetic utterances contain a wide array of implicatures, which Sperber and Wilson see as a poet's directive to her audience to expand the context.[62] In the case of poetry, the reader must work harder for meaning. As Croatto argues, a text can say many things at once, especially if it contains stylistics, but it is critical to recognize the limits the text itself provides. As such, the text of the Song does not provide for a simplistic allegory featuring God and Israel; however at the same time God and Israel are not necessarily excluded by the text. Importantly, Relevance Theory does not advocate *carte blanche* and would argue similarly to the proponents of traditional, semiotic-based hermeneutics such as Croatto:

---

60. Hippolytus in 200 CE. Longman, *Song of Songs*, 28.

61. LaCocque cites Marvin Pope, in LaCocque, "The Shulamite," 250. Some allegorical readings deal with these problems by changing the gender of the voices in translation, and/or emending the Hebrew text. Longman also concedes that the historical biblical exegesis of the Song centering on allegory might be considered *ad hoc* and lacking reason. Longman, *Song of Songs*, 37.

62. Sperber and Wilson, "Précis of Relevance," 706.

The text indicates the limit (however broad) of its own meaning. Textual polysemy does not mean simply what-you-will. A text says what it permits to be said. Its polysemy arises from its previous closure. Hence the urgency of situating it in its proper context, by means of historico-critical methods, and of exploring its capacity for the production of meaning . . . in order thus to cause its "forward" to blossom from within life.[63]

The effects created through poetic stylistics are also often more impression-oriented than knowledge-oriented. It produces mutual feeling—mood—rather than cognitive mutuality. This poetry is filled with erotic ambiguities, metaphors, similes and hyperbole. Within Relevance Theory, poetics are treated by the same scheme of comprehension as other communicative forms. Through context the audience understands when a phrase is to be taken literally or if it implies another location for meaning. The audience will select the optimally relevant meaning.

One example of this in the Song is that the hyperbolic descriptors of the *Shulamith*'s body throughout the Song of Songs form literally what Fiona Black describes as "grotesque" and "comical,"[64] a head like Carmel, a nose like a tower. Relevance Theory would not support Black's reading of grotesque absurdity in the Song. The impression conjured by the hero's imagery of the *Shulamith* in chapter 7 is not grotesque and unbalanced, but intends to communicate via metaphor her strength, elegance, health, value, smoothness, sweet taste, fragrance and earthiness. The hero then helpfully concludes his *wasf* with an explicit statement of her beauty (7:7). If one has never seen the majesty of Mt Carmel, nor the shape of a flock on its slopes, nor drunk spiced wine from a round smooth cup, one would never understand the implication; the synesthaesia invoked here. These implicatures require embedding with a sensitive awareness of the Israeli geography, agricultural produce and the quickening experience of love.

This approach presupposes a will to listen empathetically to the voice in the text. A hermeneutic of consent must be at work.[65] The consenting reader agrees to follow the voice to its origins, that is, to enter into dialogue

---

63. Croatto, *Theory of Reading*, 80.

64. Black, "Beauty or the Beast?," 311. See also Black, *The Artifice of Love*.

65. Richard Davidson bases his studies of sexuality in the Old Testament on a "hermeneutic of consent," though it is through this hermeneutic that he justifies a narrow, fundamentalist view of sexuality. It is debatable whether Davidson has a valid hermeneutic of consent or perhaps rather a hermeneutic that attempts to justify a certain kind of consent. Davidson, *Flame of Yahweh*, 3.

and work to understand what the poet meant. The reader cannot hope to follow that voice by sitting in a place of judgment on it or in judgment of the styles or methods or language it seeks to employ (though there is a valid place for critique once the premises are established). The intent behind the hero's *wasf* of chapter 7, according to Relevance Theory, seems to be something like, "I adore you and every beautiful thing I see reminds me somehow of you."

Poetry and prose are characteristically indirect and subtle forms of communication. But subtle communications can be prevalent in oral communication situations. Weak implicatures in speech can convey information or intent that would otherwise be abrupt or impertinent in a more explicit or concrete form.

Irony

Irony and other tropes are categorized in Relevance Theory as refractions of another's thoughts. Reported speech containing irony achieves relevance through its echoes from earlier communication but with a change in tone. Irony reveals the author's attitude towards a certain statement or concept in a way that is made manifest to the reader. Sperber and Wilson see the recovery of implicatures in ironic or even sarcastic statements as dependent on the recognition of the utterance as echoic, the source of the opinion echoed, and the recognition of the visual and aural cues that characterize the author's intent as ironic.[66] An example of irony in the Song of Songs may be this phrase in Song 8:12b: *You can have the thousand, Shlomo! / And the fruit-takers, two hundred!*

The echo can be located in the previous verse where the heroine recounts: *Shlomo had a vineyard . . .* which continues a thread from verse 7b: *if someone gave all the wealth in his house for love, he would gain only utter contempt*. This statement by the heroine appears to reject the wealth and power symbolised by *Shlomo* the King in order to better embrace the simplicity of love with the one she chooses, and thus making verse 8:12b an ironic in context. Relevance Theory thus provides a way to support an ironic reading in an ancient text through the location of its echo.

---

66. Sperber and Wilson, "Précis of Relevance," 708.

Biblical Interpretation

Since pragmatics is concerned with the derivation of meaning from language made by actual people in a real time and place, it is expressly applicable to biblical hermeneutics, which is the science of interpretation of biblical texts written by actual people in actual places, long, long ago. For the most part this science has maintained a traditional and inadequate theory of language though reception of modern theories of language is growing.[67] The new approach to language, evidenced in theories, like Relevance Theory, reconnects *the word* to meaningful chunks of language situated within a broader milieu and grounded in context. It is an approach to language that is able to embrace the *sui generis* of language, capable of differentiating between statements of fact and sarcasm, poetic hyperbole and literal commands, between pure description and metaphor, between opinion and insult. Relevance Theory attempts to capture this complexity of language. Its observations produce a unifying theoretical framework in the hope of providing a concrete basis for hermeneutics.

In literary communication the responsibility of the author as the creator of the text is to communicate effectively what he or she means, and the responsibility of the text's audience is to work along a "cost-effective" path to discover original meaning.

The exegete must work to understand the author's intent sometimes across thousands of years and be cognizant that non-original audiences create new meanings from texts because their own cognitive environments are unique and distant from the original communicative event.[68] While the making of new meanings from a text is creative and a valid reading practice, the priority remains to discern the intent of the text's creator and enter into genuine dialogue with that intention. In the original communicative event, the author instinctively takes into account the cognitive environment of the author's intended audience and manipulates language via innate knowledge

---

67. Thiselton goes as far to say the exegete ignores the new linguistics at "his" peril. Thiselton, "Semantics," 100.

68. This is an important principle in Relevance theory for biblical interpretation. When we read a text displaced in time and setting we bring to it our own environment of experience and knowledge. A text will mean different things to different groups. Particular individuals in the modern audience of the Song will identify authentically with different themes, i.e., the vulnerability of women, the plight of star-crossed lovers, the male hegemony, the importance of family. The exegete must work to recreate that initial cognitive environment that birthed the Song.

of that environment in order to inform and impact the reader somehow with the communication.

In biblical hermeneutics, Relevance Theory does not replace the traditional or conventional hermeneutical methodologies but provides a framework in which they may cooperate to provide the often elusive meaning housed in the linguistic code of the Bible. As Stephen Pattemore aptly demonstrates, Relevance Theory elevates the text to the category of *real communication event* and this in itself on the basis of consent.[69] The text is as it is.

Relevance Theory also provides a refreshingly detailed and explicit definition for context as *mutual cognitive environment* so that analysis of the text is guided by an understanding of what the mutual cognitive environment was for the author and the author's intended audience and how that environment evolves as the text unfolds. The mutual cognitive environment first and foremost is located by co-text. Even in the contemporary readings of the Song, what the author has written earlier in the text continues to impact subsequent lines text which also informs or reforms the reader's understanding of it. Finally, Relevance Theory limits the scope of the mutual cognitive environment. The search for implicatures or echoes in the text delimits according to the principle that the most likely interpretation is the one that the primary audience would have expected, and thus most likely the intention of the author. This is the principle of *Occam's Razor*: "*Entia non sunt multiplicanda, praeter necessitatem*: One should not increase, beyond what is necessary, the number of entities required to explain anything," or, in other words and in our context, the simpler the interpretation, the more likely it is correct.[70]

The exegete's task is to extract the most authentic meaning from the text. Relevance Theory argues that hermeneutics should embrace the whole communicative process, which includes sociolinguistic and pragmatic factors. If a secondary audience attempts to step into the shoes of the primary audience and mimic as best as possible their process of comprehension, the range of possible interpretations narrows considerably.

When doing hermeneutical work from the perspective of Relevance Theory we necessarily ask the questions "To whom did the author think they were writing?" and, "How did that audience affect the way in which

---

69. Such as: textual criticism, historical-critical analysis, discourse analysis, historical-sociological analysis and rhetorical criticism. Pattemore, "Relevance Theory," 41.

70. Molé, "Occam's Razor Cuts Both Ways."

the author writes: the implication, connotations, suggestions, the way the author turns her words in order to impact the target audience?" Often, unfortunately, we have as little clear access to the primary audience as we do the author. The difficulty in reading biblical texts in context is determining who the author and intended audience were. Much must be discerned from historical, archaeological, sociological, and anthropological sources.

There are further complications beyond provenance. Biblical texts no longer stand alone, but come under the auspices of the canon and contribute to an evolving story of God and the world. These texts are housed in the new discursive space of the Judeo-Christian canons, and therefore to some degree the redactors and translators become influential forces, obstructing rather than facilitating a sense of the original authorial intent. In some cases the text has moved very far from its original milieu. However, it is not impossible to re-embed some or much of the lost context with forensic exploration.

Histories of reception impact the cognitive-cultural space in which we find a text. Ancient and biblical texts are unique in that while they originate from a distinct communication event, they are also the end point of a progressive one, the end of an evolutionary process embodying all the contextual environments that punctuated its historical development. These texts could be said to be the result of discourse over time. Croatto writes regarding the fluidity of meaning in biblical texts:

> All discourse—as the attempt to say something to someone about something—requires a *contextual* closure [culturally and literally] to render it intelligible. Otherwise it is not a message. . . . [the Bible] was written by and for the Hebrew people. Only by way of profound re-readings did it come to be the book of the first Christians, in a restricted geographical area . . .[71]

---

71. Croatto, *Theory of Reading*, 79.

Pardes: The Essence of Communication

Noam Chomsky eloquently identifies human language as the defining quality of humanity: "When we study human language, we are approaching what some might call the 'human essence,' the distinctive qualities of mind that are, so far as we know, unique to man."[72] While many life forms also communicate there are no other creatures with the mental faculties enabling them to create messages with such a range of expression, depth and subject, nuance and allusion. The human spirit cannot survive without communication. Humans explain thoughts, express emotions and share dreams through media of communication. Moreover, language and communication is essential to human development.

In biblical literature the very first recorded "communication act" was also an act of physical creation—the Creator, the parent of humanity, spoke, and created light in Genesis (1:3b). Language was first creative:

יהי אור

Communication, according to the Genesis text, was a basic need of the newly created 'adam and the narrator described the "aloneness" of that first human who was unable to share with anyone like himself, his experiences of this new world. The negative power of language to deceive, corrupt and steal innocence was also an early event in this same text. Language could destroy.

> He said to the woman, "Did God really say: You shall not eat of every tree of the garden?" (Gen 3:1)

Language could also redeem: to bind and seal a promise, affirm belief and appeal to the heights of human experience. Even two thousand years or more since its appearance, the language of the Hebrew Bible still emanates a potency that inspires and awakens a reader. Language has always held the power to transform.

> Set me as a seal upon your heart
> A seal upon your arm
> For love is as vehement as death
> Its passion as relentless as Sheol
> A radiant flaming fire (Song 8:6)

---

72. Chomsky, *Language and Mind*, 100.

Pardes: A Framework

From the beginning of biblical time, language, in all its forms, has been a potent, powerful essence that deeply affects humanity and influences the course of history. Evidencing this in the field of biblical studies, is that ancient words long since said, still have a force that causes transformation of the mind of the reader. It is this quality of language that biblical scholars and linguists—religious and secular—have tried to adequately explain.

Relevance Theory is a pragmatic approach that claims to understand the dynamic nature of language as communication earthed in context. Relevance Theory captures the phenomena of real language at both physical and cognitive levels and accommodates the broad spectrum of communication events: from love whispers to literature. While not replacing the traditional approach to language, Relevance Theory complements and incorporates traditional and modern approaches into its explanation of the communication event. Its treatment of language as such is holistic where traditional approaches have been found to be constrained and detached.

Relevance Theory is a theory of language and as such it is primarily descriptive, but it has been applied successfully to biblical studies and bible translation.[73] The advantage of Relevance Theory for hermeneutics is that it provides a robust understanding of context as a key factor in exegesis. In doing this, Relevance Theory provides a framework in which to situate a text, an explanation of how that framework conforms to the text as it unfolds, and how that framework intersects with the text to provide meaning. Relevance Theory also offers a way of delimiting the many interpretations offered by scholars for any particular text. Relevance Theory above all values the text as a unique communiqué from an author, whose intent was to successfully communicate with the intended audience. Relevance Theory does not prioritize infinitely regressive readings, extreme deconstruction or hermeneutics of suspicion but offers a theoretically bounded plane within which the meaning of a text might be found; delimiting rather than indiscriminate.

The study of human language has progressed in its quest to discern more descriptively the workings of human communication that produces at its heights such genius of transformative literature as the scroll of the Song of Songs. Relevance Theory represents in modern linguistics, a giant leap forward in adequately delineating the processes of communication.

---

73. Gutt demonstrates the significance of Relevance Theory for Bible Translation in *Relevance Theory*. Stephen Pattemore successfully applied Relevance Theory to the book of Revelation. Pattemore, *The People of God*.

Earthing the Cosmic Queen

In the reading of ancient literature it is applied in order to better elucidate authorial intent. In biblical literature it is found to be consequential in the interpretation of challenging texts, reaffirming the humanity (and thus the divinity) of these communication events.

> O woman
> Garden dweller!
> Comrades listen for your voice
> Let me hear it! (Song 8:13)

2

Peshat: A Discourse Analysis

There are many levels and complexities to the Song of Songs. It is not as simple as to call it a song like any other; neither is it a simple narrative, nor does it progress according to the expectations of drama. There is certainly active debate regarding the structure or unity of the Song as a whole and there are certainly differing views of its degree of coherence. Athalya Brenner recalls from her childhood the various old Hebrew tunes that accompany bits and pieces of the Song's text and the excerpts found in liturgy.[1] Not even in Jewish folk music is it sung as an entire song. Some call it an anthology of poems, like Marcia Falk, who is one of many prominent readers of the Song who see not one but thirty-one poems.[2] Tremper Longman III finds a middle (though slightly tenuous) place with his opinion that it is "a single song composed of many different songs."[3] Alicia Ostriker passionately writes in her essay, "Holy of Holies," that this song is absolutely unique among the texts of the Bible and thus unclassifiable.[4]

---

1. Brenner, "'My' Song of Songs," 157–58.
2. Falk, *The Song of Songs*, xix.
3. Longman, *Song of Songs*, 55.
4. Ostriker, "A Holy of Holies," 50.

Earthing the Cosmic Queen

I had first considered the Song perhaps a generational work,[5] but one finding coherence from its overarching macrostructure.[6] After a detailed analysis of the Song, and the evidence of the consistency of voice behind the Song, and the clever and consistent usage of creation motifs, the notion of a sole author seems more probable.[7] This poet has created a wondrously ornate story through shifting prose.[8]

The Song of Songs is a whole, rather than a collection, though a unique and whole text that appears to subvert and elude all expectations of form and style. The text's ethereal quality is lost if dismembered into pieces. Even in the text's disjointedness it has a *je ne sais quoi* vitality.[9] The Song of Songs' metanarrative is surprisingly clear and voiced repeatedly. The poet leaves even the modern audience burning through a masterful execution of verbal expression.

The study of the surface level of a biblical text according to the kabbalistic framework exemplified by the Zohar is called *Peshat*. This chapter seeks to explore the *peshat* level of the Song of Songs but reading with modern discourse analysis rather than the reading practiced by the medieval kabbalist. The discourse analysis highlights the unifying structural features. It describes the literary topography of the Song of Songs and that is inherently causative in terms of producing meaning. Chapter 3 will explore an evolved *Remez-Derasha* reading, a sociolinguistic exploration that pursues intertextual echoes and implicatures.

Firstly to establish the framework, text, translation and provenance...

---

5. By "generational" I mean a composite piece contributed to by a number of authors who as in "fan fiction" write improvisations in accordance with the genre and context outlined in the earliest portions of the Song. The final appearance being the work of a gifted editor in late post-exilic times. The result would be a very esoteric piece of writing that is timeless in a much more concrete way than many texts. It would truly belong to many different stages of Israel's development. However, the evidence for a single voice is too strong in my opinion.

6. Wendland, "Seeking the Path," 44.

7. This consistency of voice and unity of theme in the Song is strong evidence for a single author. See also Landy, "The Song of Songs," 315–16.

8. In this image of the poet as a woman, I wholeheartedly agree with LaCocque, "The Shulamite," 241–44, who provides a persuasive rationale based on both biblical precedent of women singers and comparative Egyptian evidence of the same.

9. See also Landy, "The Song of Songs," 315–16, and LaCocque, "The Shulamite," 236.

Peshat: A Discourse Analysis

The Theoretical Framework

Following the discussion of Relevance Theory in chapter 1, the concept of *cognitive environment* and more precisely *mutual cognitive environment* is of critical importance to examining communication events like text from the Relevance theoretic perspective. As Stephen Pattemore points out, a relevance-sensitive methodology elucidates the thought-processes of the author.[10] The author's purpose is prioritized in the study. Educated assumptions about the author's original audience are employed. Pattemore suggests a 6-fold process: establish the text, elucidate the discourse structure, identify the issue (the moment or *crisis* that produced the communication), describe the cognitive environments, evaluate the accessibility of cognitive environments, and finally interpret the text within prioritized contexts.[11] With some innovations, these are the tasks in mind as I embark on a journey to locate the poet through her own words.

The Text

The Hebrew text of the Song of Songs used in this study is the Masoretic Text without emendations.[12] I have analyzed the text without the imposition of chapter and verse. There are few significant differences between the Masoretic Text and the Septuagint.[13] The Vulgate and the Peshitta essentially relate to the Septuagint.[14] The Targum to the Song of Songs is an explicitly allegorical adaption. Four Qumran scrolls of the Song exist and date to the Roman period.[15] Two of these scrolls seem to omit deliberately

---

10. Pattemore, *The People of God*, 49–50.

11. Ibid., 48–50.

12. The primary reference for the Hebrew text is that of the Leningrad codex as edited and presented by, Elliger et al., *Biblia Hebraica Stuttgartensia*. I do not present the Masoretic vowel points in my reproductions of the MT here.

13. I might note however that the Septuagint uses the word *agapè* consistently throughout (thanks to my student Rachel Wilson for drawing my attention to this). From the context of the Song's clearly erotic focus the "earthy" erotic dimension allowable in the Hebrew *ahavah* might be diminished in this possibly "purist" Greek equivalent. In the context of the Song, the Greek word *eros* may better connote the meaning of *ahavah*. On *eros* and *agapè* in the Song, see also LaCocque, "The Shulamite," 251.

14. Pope, *Song of Songs*, 20.

15. 30 BCE– 70 CE. Abegg et al., *The Dead Sea Scrolls Bible*, 612.

the erotic poetry from 4:7 to 6:11.[16] Of the portions remaining of the Song, Song 6:12 and 7:9 are examples of minor textual discrepancies.[17]

Translation

There are many choices to make in translation and I have worked to closely align my translation with the text as it exists in the traditional Hebrew text. However, I have sought to add context-sensitive information, bracketed, where translation fails to fully represent the original language. This embedded material is signalled by the poet and in agreement with the apparent train of thought, and that I find must be added to the translation in order to aid the modern reader. The vision has been to create a translation that will faithfully present the poet's voice to a modern reader, one that will create in the reader cognitive representations that are more closely related to original intent and thus enable untrammelled dialogue with words long since sung.[18]

The other English translation that skilfully reflects the spirit and meter of the Song while retaining the grammar and vocabulary is that of Ariel and Chana Bloch.[19] I have noted where I employ their translations. The Bloch translation is a dynamic translation that attempts to capture other stylistics such as plays on words. Their English translation has been very helpful in my reading of the Song. Carey Ellen Walsh has been particularly persuasive in her approach to the Song as concerning *desire* and this has impacted my reading greatly.[20]

---

16. Ibid. The question is why the section was omitted and whether this was the true condition of the old scrolls from which they copied. If the missing portions of the Song did exist at that time, what the Qumran scribes saw in the missing sections clearly disturbed them. This may reveal the way that at least this group interpreted those portions of the Song at the time. Obviously allegorizing the Song as the rabbinic tradition did was not sufficient. Abegg et al. see the raw eroticism of the missing parts as the most probable reason for omission. I wonder however if concerns over "idolatry" may in fact be the real reason. The omission contains *wasf* of the man and woman that implicitly invoke stone gods. What did they see?

17. Exum challenges the text at points using the Qumran remnants of the Song as a comparison. She views the Masoretic Text at 6:12 and 7:9 as corruptions. Exum, *Song of Songs*, 28.

18. Vanhoozer recalls Emily Dickinson on this note, and he is correct, "A word is dead / when it is said / some say / I say it just / begins to live / that day" in Vanhoozer, "From Speech Acts to Scripture," 1.

19. Bloch and Bloch, *The Song of Songs*.

20. Several scholars have particularly influenced my reading and translation of the

Peshat: A Discourse Analysis

Provenance

The date of the Song is as elusive as the unity of its text, as its storyline. Marvin Pope has written an encyclopaedic work on the Song of Songs listing all manner of potential *Sitze im Leben* for the Song.[21] Accordingly, Pope gives grounds for "the oldest and youngest estimates" of its age.[22] The compilation and final redaction of the text is more than likely to be of a late provenance, perhaps the postexilic period.[23] Its strong connection with the wisdom writings could also justify a postexilic development.[24]

Some parts of the Song seem to reflect on the period of King Solomon's rule, such as the scene where he is crowned (3:11), which might make the Song originally a product from his reign or soon after. There are some parts of the Song, which seem too politically indiscreet to be Solomonic,[25] and as such seem unlikely to find their provenance during Solomon's powerful reign.[26]

There are texts in the Song that appear ancient and these may point to the pioneering period of Israel where women's roles in society may have

---

Song of Songs. Of note is the fascinating reading from Walsh, *Exquisite Desire*. Keel has been significant in broadening my understanding of ANE mythology with respect to the Song of Songs, Keel, *The Song of Songs*. Finally Matthew Fox's review of Egyptian love poetry was also profoundly transformative in my approach to the Song. Fox, *The Song of Songs and the Ancient Egyptian Love Songs*.

21. Pope, *Song of Songs*, 22–33.

22. Ibid., 27. For example, Tirzah, the capital of the Northern kingdom under Jeroboam, is indicative of a post-Solomonic age.

23. Many argue a young age due to the presence of Aramaisms and Greek loan words. See Murphy, *The Song of Songs*, 4.

24. Fee and Stuart see strong stylistic connections between Song 8:7 and the Proverbs. Fee and Stuart, *How to Read the Bible for All Its Worth*.

25. In chapter 8 of the Song, the heroine seems to mock *Shlomo* for his material success but impoverished experience of love. Though in other parts of the Song he seems to be lauded, i.e., "Solomon's palanquin" . . . the people of the city love him. Is this the building of irony in the Song?

26. Therefore logically at least that part of the Song must be later than *Shlomo*'s rule during a time when incendiary comments about Israel's king were not regarded as treason. The prophets and people held *Shlomo* in high regard for centuries, and he was also the patron of the post-exilic wisdom writings. His reign is part of the golden memory of Israel but his faults and failings were also part of that memory. It is difficult to delineate an age where the general populace might have been jaded concerning these old kings. Hebrew women on the other hand may have had more reasons to explore the irony of his patronage of love songs and poetry.

been more publicly influential.[27] This is also a time of greater affinity with the lyrics and legends of Canaanite mythology.[28] The Song may provide allusions to what may have been a time of Egyptian ascendancy in the Near East (late Bronze to early Iron Age). This was a time before the monarchy. According to Carol Meyers, the norms for men and women changed radically with the development of Israel and Judah into kingdoms.[29] Yet in other places and if silence speaks volumes, the patriarchal yoke seems to be the frame from which the *Shulamith* bursts.

Thus, the poem does not easily reveal her age but as Alicia Ostriker notes, this lends a timeless quality to the Song.[30] The Song has a long memory, and all at once she is contemporary, primeval, ancient and antique.[31] The Song is difficult to be pin down and this is part of the text's charm. She seems to obey no rules. In the context of the range of scenarios in which the Song may had its provenance, the most important traces come from the text's own internal geography.

It is feasible to assume that much of the Song indicates a Judean poet and by extension a Judean audience. In terms of Relevance Theory, in order to appreciate the relevance of the communication, the original audience must have belonged to, or be cognizant of, the same culture and heritage

27. That is, greater value placed on the childbearing qualities of women. Carol Meyers identifies the settlement period of the Judean hills as a period where women enjoyed greater respect and autonomy. This is perhaps due to the crucial and honored role they play in birthing laborers and warriors, "a mother in Israel" (2 Sam 20:19; Judg 5:7). The chapter 6 refrain "daunting as the stars" (also here the woman is recounted as overwhelming, blazing, breath-taking, in chapter 7 she is towering, proud) is less likely to find its provenance in the later urban, civilized periods where concurrent images of women reflected periodically in some of the prophetic books showed disdain. Amos 4:1 we see the women of Israel described as "cows of Bashan." In Hosea we see the humiliation of Gomer in response to her adultery. She is figuratively the people of Israel. The prophets regularly describe Israel/Judah/Jerusalem as a prostituted woman. Ezek 16:17; Hos 4:15; Jer 2:20 et al. Or a divorced, shamed woman: Isa 50:1; Jer 50:12 et al. Shamed, violated and naked young woman: Lam 1:8; Ezek 16:7; Hos 2:3 et al.; Meyers, *Discovering Eve: Ancient Israelite Women in Context*, 165. Keel supports this notion also recalling the freedom of women in an older age (several of the matriarchs) to meet men by the well without consequence. i.e., Rivkah, Rachel, Zipporah, Gen 24:15, 29:10; Exod 2:16; Keel, *The Song of Songs*, 120.

28. Especially the "my sister, my bride" poems in chapter 4. See Keel, *The Song of Songs*, 155.

29. Meyers, *Discovering Eve*, 191.

30. Ostriker, "A Holy of Holies," 40.

31. "Antique" denotes the period of Roman suzerainty in Israel, the period when much of the apocalyptic literature was written.

of the poet. The familiar sounds, smells and sights of Israel and especially southern Israel are scattered throughout the text. The mutual cognitive environment of the audience also must include the Torah and the legends of the patriarchs, as many of the weak implicatures in the story are not grasped by anything less than a fluency in this discursive cultural space, from Abraham to Judah's sons, to the annals of the kings.

LaCocque emphatically sees a woman-poet at work in the Song. I concur. The poet has such a strong affinity with the *ways of women* and the women's perspectives and though not impossible, it is very difficult to imagine such woman-centred conceptions coming from the sphere of the priestly urban elite. LaCocque produces comparative archaeological evidence from Egypt where women worked professionally in music and particularly writing and performing songs.[32] There is a similar precedent in Israel, with women participating in love songs, war songs and dirges.[33] This femininity pervasive in the Song emerges strongly in the discourse analysis. I emphasize this quality throughout by applying a feminine pronoun to both poet and song.[34]

Nevertheless, that the scroll of the Song of Songs has been preserved and placed in the canon shows the positive reception and inherent value of the text to subsequent generations of Jews. However, the text did not come into the canon without a struggle. Early Rabbinic material finds the Song in the centre of debate in the great synagogue and Akiba, her champion. Rabbi Akiba[35] by all accounts had to prove the case for the canonization of the Song in front of his peers, reminding them that the Song had "always

---

32. LaCocque, "The Shulamite," 241–44.

33. Such biblical characters abound, like Miriam, Deborah, Hannah (1 Sam 18:6–7; Exod 15:20; Judg 4:9;, Ps 68:12; Isa 37:22; Jer 38:22).

34. There are many clues suggesting woman-authorship of the Song but no irrefutable evidence. LaCocque's argument is persuasive however and with that I make an intuitive decision regarding the author's gender. LaCocque, "The Shulamite," 241–44.

35. Akiba was the Rabbi who famously entered *pardes* which is "orchard" in Hebrew but an acronym that stands for the Jewish mystical hermeneutic: *peshat, remez, derasha* and *sodh*, but also mystically, the Torah or Tanakh, the word of God, that is told of in Proverbs as a tree of life and considered by devout Jews a garden of delight. He journeyed to the heavenly garden with three others, but in the vignette he is the only sage who had sufficient purity of heart to enter and leave the heavenly garden whole. The other three were lost in different ways: insanity, atheism and death. Sperling, "Jewish Mysticism," 150–51.

made hands unclean," i.e., was a holy book, famously describing it as the "holy of holies."[36]

Discourse Structure

I wanted the text to speak for itself and so I removed chapter and verse breaks and worked through the Song phrase by phrase, beginning the journey of an informed and empathic unpacking of the Song's discourse. Next I follow closely any threads or conceptual flows, which are evidence of the poet's intent.

Characteristically, poetry is written with ideas outworked in progression, though in the genre of the poetic these communications are vastly more subtle and allusive that in concrete narrative. These layers of thought ("dishevelled" tendrils in the Song) are traceable even though they are tenuous. Sometimes the poet returns and builds on earlier ideas. Sometimes the poet pushes forward into new territory or moves out laterally. It is important to recognize these as markers in a text that attest to the developing topography of the poet's panorama. The Song is deceptively whimsical at a structural and organizational level, toing-and-froing between speakers, genders, groups and unspecified participants. There is both cacophony and harmony as groups and speakers burst in, seemingly uninvited, and then with delicate artistry, the Song picks up the scattered threads and ties them in. The Song quickly moves between settings, scenes and scenarios. This is the Song as we have it.

Ernst Wendland has also discussed the Song of Songs in terms of a discourse analysis and structure.[37] Though Wendland comes to the Song from a different perspective, he does similarly draw attention to the loose chiastic structures that give certain meaningfulness and belonging to all the parts of this multidimensional work. I agree that in amongst all this chaotic and heady verse there are flags that provide complex connections. I have highlighted these markers in the discourse analysis.

---

36. *T. Sanh.* 12.10 quoted in Murphy, *The Song of Songs*, 13; also in *M. Yad.* 3:5 cited in Wendland, "Seeking the Path," 52.

37. Wendland, "Seeking the Path," 13–59.

Superstructure

In the discourse analysis, I locate seven significant and progressive sites in the poet's discourse within the Song of Songs. These are listed sequentially as they also appear in the text: firstly, The Entreaties, then, The *Wasf*, The Daughters, Royalty, The Brothers, Losing and Finding, and finally, at the text's outer reaches, The Garden. These locales that are repeatedly visited by the poet throughout the Song and each subsequent stich of poetry can be aligned to these themes via either content or form (i.e., entreaty). Progressively throughout the Song the locales of the poet's focus begin to intersect even in single lines, or in a single phrase. Some stichs could be equally aligned with two or more sites and I have, in these circumstances, chosen the locale or platform that best fits considering the evidence in prior and subsequent text. The rhythmic movement of the Song between these sites of the poet's focus becomes manifest as the discourse progresses. It is like the ebb and flow of the tides, but also, in some places in the text the movement is jolting and disorienting. The Song of Songs moves between entreaty and the garden no less than 15 times throughout the entire work. A number of these movements are buoyed or underscored by other literary devices such as a series of refrains, or repeated concepts.[38]

The entire discourse in general has three interconnecting and overlapping moods or states. The mood of conflict or oppression (or repression) pervades the Song and emerges concretely in several places. This conflict adds the important tension in the Song that makes the text so emotionally engaging. The state of struggle: the escaping, the awakening, the bursting through, the yearning, the recognizing, the dreaming, losing, looking for and finding is the primary state of the Song.[39] Finally the state of fulfilment, *shalom*, completeness, the "coming home" found in the garden scenes seems to indicate an almost tangible return to Eden, and this must be recognized. However, these returns are in brief snatches and the reader is almost relieved of the building anticipation, but then left without satiation. The reader feels, with the players, that true realized *shalom* is always, already somewhere else, perhaps over the mountains that seemed to encircle the heroine. The Song, in a series of chiasms and inclusio, moves between suppression, struggle, and actualization. This movement is strongly evident in the shape of the discourse structure. The Song also progresses forward

---

38. Wendland labels these "recursions." Wendland, "Seeking the Path," 15.
39. Walsh, *Exquisite Desire*, 4.

in these three main themes of suppression, struggle and actualization with the addition of new scenarios, new ideas or old scenarios with alternate outcomes. Throughout the Song of Songs the intensity of the suppression, the struggle and grasping towards actualization grows.

While the structure I have outlined gives the text unity, it does not give it predictability and seems to purposefully avoid providing a singular, concrete interpretation. Though it might be said that phrases like *I would descend into the walnut garden* seem to have as rich innuendo for us now as it might have done for the intended audience. The Song of Songs challenges her readers with mythic, earthy and timeless truths about the human condition. As a song that seems to move effortlessly through the centuries, her audience moves too through a series of foci spanning the history of Judah (and Israel). Due to this chronological expansiveness, complex and myriad interpretations seem an inherent product of reading the Song. The Song of Songs was a Hebrew song/poem meant for a Hebrew audience but it embraces a generic human condition. The text touches us all. Authorship and whatever redaction may have occurred bring a transcendence to the Song that is not necessarily out of the scope of the poet's intent.[40] The two lovers could embody any of the many of the lovers in Hebrew scripture and history. They are a mythical couple in that sense. She is potentially any woman. He is potentially any man. This mythic quality enables the Song to reach out of its pages and touch the reader. The poet seems to write with all of us in mind.

Reading the Discourse Analysis

The platforms in the Song move from left to right, in the order that the poet has them first appear in the Song. The Song develops vertically line by line; each line builds on the last and thus growing in meaning. Each subsequent line is aligned with the thematic focus that best represents the substance of the stich. In this way reflections on or developments of earlier ideas are recognized as well as movements towards new ideas. Throughout the Song each of the seven sites develop significantly.

---

40. Most scholars see the Song as having some history of redaction, however I agree with Landy and LaCocque that this song seems too consistent in its voice to have been heavily reworked or to be the production of generations of authors. Landy, "The Song of Songs," 516 and LaCocque, "The Shulamite," 241–44.

Peshat: A Discourse Analysis

Title	Entreaties	You are	Daughters	Royalty	Brothers	Lost/Found	Garden
0	1	2	3	4	5	6	7

The Song of Songs, of Solomon
        Kiss me, make me drunk with your kisses!
              Your sweet loving is better than wine
              You are fragrant,
              You are myrrh and aloes
                  All the young women want you
        Take me by the hand, let us run [together]!
                     My lover, my king
                     Has brought me into his chambers
        We will laugh you and I,
        And count each kiss better than wine
                Every one of them want you
              I am dark, daughters of Jerusalem,
              And I am beautiful!
              Dark as the tents of Kedar,
              Lavish as Solomon's tapestries
              Do not see me as dark; the sun has stared at me
                     My brothers were angry at me
                     They made me guard the vineyard
                     I have not guarded my own

Figure 2: Discourse analysis for verses 1:1–6

It is not a light task to unpack an ancient poet's thinking processes. Some parts of the Song are disjointed. The introduction of new foci or sudden recursions to other locales, seem purposefully jolting. Some movements between ideas are incredibly rapid. Other parts of the Song flow and move between thoughts smoothly. The to-and-fro movements of the poet through her sites of focus bring structure to the Song and a sense of purpose and direction. Yet the Song retains an air of mystery and unpredictability that makes it such a reservoir of discovery and surprise for the audience. Othmar Keel notes this movement as psychological. There is changing

Earthing the Cosmic Queen

consciousness within the Song.[41] The representation of these movements as a series of dream sequences is also a very apt description.

The discourse analysis

Superscription

The Song begins with the superscription, which as a probable addition to the original text I mark as level 0. One might say the superscription is rather like a hyperlink into the portal of the Song. It is uncharacteristically straightforward (as far as the rest of the Song goes) but it is a precipice edge and the rest of the Song follows like a downward plunge.

The superscript gives the title of the work: *the Song of Songs,* and attributes it to the genre of *Shlomo*. However as Rabbi Nosson Scherman notes, the name itself could point, beyond Solomon the man, to the Holy One: "to Him to whom *Shalom* belongs."[42]

שיר השירים אשר לשלמה

So it is perhaps not a straightforward superscription at all. *Shalom* is very much the quest of the Song. This *shalom* is found in the secret world of the two lovers. That the superscript is a lost key might in fact be significant. The Song seems to be as much about the yearning for *shalom* as about anything.

Entreaties

The entreaties are level 1 of the discourse analysis I propose. In general, these entreaties are identifiable by their volitional mood. We recognize them grammatically as cohortatives, imperatives and jussives.[43] The strongest volitional is the imperative: a command, desire, or will expressed directly by one to another, the second person. The jussive is the softest of the

---

41. Keel, *The Song of Songs*, 119.

42. Rashi recognized that in other instances, i.e., Proverbs and Ecclesiastes, *Shlomo* is recognized as *ben David* however in the Song this is omitted. Rashi believed it pointed to another *Shlomo*: שלו מלך שהשלום [the King to whom peace belongs]. This he writes in his allegorical interpretation. Scherman, *Tanach*, 1682 (note 1:1).

43. Ross, *Biblical Hebrew*, 149–51.

Peshat: A Discourse Analysis

volitionals and it is a desire expressed by one towards another, not present, in the third or fourth person. The cohortative is not nearly as strong as the imperative and yet stronger than the jussive. It is a desire or yearning expressed by one to oneself. It often takes the form in poetry or dramatic literature as an actor's or character's interior monologue or soliloquy.

Song 1:2

The poet begins in the volitional mood with the first entreaty a soft jussive spoken by the heroine. The mood quickly strengthens to second person in the next phrase:

ישקני מנשיקות פיהו

כי טובים דדיך מיין

> Let him kiss me
> With the kisses of his mouth
> For **your** lovemaking is exquisite
> Better than wine

The jussive used here in the first real line of the Song is significant. It gives what prevails through the rest of the Song as the unearthly quality of the hero. We want to ask: "Is he a dream or real?" He so often seems intangible, often absent in the brief narratives. The movement between parts of speech is significant and tantalizing in this couplet. The heroine as first person expresses her desire for her hero in third person in the first half of the couplet as he was not present, but the poet then draws the audience suddenly into an intimate space (almost too close) with a sudden turn to bring the hero into second person: your *lovemaking [dodeka]*.[44]

Song 1:4

משכני אחריך נרוצה

While the poet then plunges into a series of epithets regarding the hero's earthy, wonderful smell so much so that even his name conjures it up. The

---

44. This sort of switching between persons is not unusual in Hebrew. The book of Isaiah in the servant songs switches between second person, third person, and third person plural when describing the servant i.e., Isa 41–53. Note Clines, *I, He, We, and They*.

Earthing the Cosmic Queen

scene ends with her cohortatives, *Bring me after you, let's run*, or as the Blochs have it, "Take me by the hand, let's run together!"[45] The first part of the Song is very much about the heroine's desire or will. This particular entreaty divulges the first hint of struggle. The lovers must run, but run from what?

הביאני המלך חדריו

נגילה ונשמחה בך נזכירה דדיך מיין

The poet turns again mid-verse and introduces the lover in the third person as king, *haMelek: he has brought me, the King, to his suite*, but just as quickly turns to first person (plural) *We will love and laugh [nigilah]/together/[even] to imagine your lovemaking is much better than wine.* This stich does not express the volitional mood but seems very much part of the poet's present consideration.

From this point, the poet's gaze widens introducing new locales and themes. It is now not until Song 2:8 that the poet returns to entreaty. In this case, it is an entreaty perhaps whispered only to herself but signals to her reader to listen and to look.

Song 2:8–9

קול דודי הינה-זה בא

מדלג על ההרים מקפץ על הגבעות

דומה דודי לצבי או לעפר האילים

> The voice of my lover . . .
> Behold this! He comes!
> Springing on the mountains
> Skipping on the hills
> My lover resembling a gazelle
> A young stag . . .

She can clearly see her lover coming. Does she calls this out loud, announcing this to the entire household? Perhaps it is the quiet voice of the heroine's heart. Her hero is leaping on the mountains, bounding on the hills. Do "we" see him too? He is so real to her. He may not seem to jump that high for

---

45. Bloch and Bloch, *The Song of Songs*, 45.

Peshat: A Discourse Analysis

us but we have empathy for her emotion. Suddenly the audience's response seems not to matter as reality fades away, and the poet draws the reader, merges us, into her chaotic, personal world.[46] The poet has the *Shulamith* speak in the present tense. The time is imminent. It is happening now. Now is the most important time in the world.

This meeting continues to a climax; a Shakespearean tryst.

הנה-זה עומד אחר כתלנו

משגיח מן-החלנות מציץ מן-החרכים:

Oh! [And now] he stands outside our wall [of stone]
[His eyes] searching through the casement
Peering up through the fretwork

The poet has us present as a witness to the heroine's joy. Her lover stands outside her upper casement window. Like the balcony scene from Shakespeare's *Romeo and Juliet* she is hidden from view.[47]

Song 2:10

We have empathy for her as she monologues: *he calls, my love / and speaks to me*

---

46. Rather than consistently calling the woman in the Song "the woman" or "the lover" I have chosen to call her "the heroine," as she is in the eyes of the poet, or *the Shulamith*, as she is called in chapter 7. This nomenclature "*Shulamith*" occurs only twice in the Song of Songs but is clearly representative of the personality and desire of the heroine—which is not just love nor *eros* but *shalom*. I would also like to add that while the Song seems to be speaking of a single heroine, it may not necessarily be same woman. She may be embodied by many of the matriarchs of Israel i.e., Eve, Sarah, Rebecca, Rachel, but also the famous "King's women," such as Bathsheba, Pharaoh's daughter, the Queen of Sheba, Avishag, Michal, and Abigail. There are cues that lead us to all of them. This is not necessarily an obstacle in the Song. The great artistry in the Song, the way it coheres, makes us believe she is every woman, Woman. That means that the reader also is drawn into the character of the heroine vicariously.

47. Ancient Hebrew homes are windowless on the ground floor. The entire wall was of stone and sealed with plaster. Upper storeys and the roof area may have windows but these are covered by a decorative lattice-shutter or grille. It was this kind of lattice through which Jezebel leaned out and looked through, and then was famously thrown out in 2 Kings 9:30ff. Ariel and Chana Bloch have their hero looking through stonework gaps. I think this is a wealthy family house, and believe, on the basis of the emphasis on "looking down" in the verses that follow, that an upper casement window is in the author's mind. Bloch and Bloch, *The Song of Songs*, 59.

Earthing the Cosmic Queen

ענה דודי ואמר לי

"We" experience the heroine's emotion as we look through her eyes and are vicariously entreated by him.

קומי לך רעיתי יפתי ולכי-לך:

Rise up! Walk!
My darling friend, my beauty
And come away . . .

Once again the entreaty is a call to come, come away from. The poet has this Shakespearean Romeo call to her to come down, come away. Is he there as a bona fide fiancé or is he a true Romeo, a star-crossed lover without familial consent? The poet does not reveal his position or association to the heroine's family, whether his pursuit of the heroine is legitimate. However, implicitly there is urgency in his entreaty that she must go, walk, journey, step out to realize her dream but also hints that there are agents within her world who would prevent her.

Song 2:11–13a

The poet has the hero present an argument to encourage his paramour to come down and go with him. He presents his case that, as in spring, their love is ripening like the fruit and flowers, and in the process of birthing new life.

כי-הנה הסתו עבר הגשם חלף חלך לו:

הנצנים נראו בארץ

עת הזמיר הגיע

וקול התור נשמע בארצינו:

התאנה חנתה פגיה

והגפנים סמדר נתנו ריח . . .

Winter is over
[in its steps] the rains too have passed by and gone
Wildflowers appear on the earth
Now the time of birdsong is beginning
The voice of the turtledove is heard in our land

The green fruit of the fig is turning
And the fragrant vine blossoms breathe . . .

Song 2:13b

This entreaty strengthens with an inclusio. It repeats almost phrase for phrase the first line (2:10b).

קומי לכי [לך] רעיתי יפתי ולכי לך:

Rise up and walk [to me]
My friend, my beauty
Step out

Song 2:14

Her hero describes her as a small bird perched between the rocks in the cliffs above the valley. Is she unsure or afraid? Why? She like a "Juliet" is only just visible from her upper window, not far away and perhaps just above him. But to her "Romeo" she couldn't be further away. She is like a tiny bird high on a rocky jut of mountain. The poet ensures we see her through his eyes. The poet keeps us seeing her through his perspective and he speaks again to the *Shulamith* and continues his entreaty:

הראיני את-מראיך
השמיני את-קולך
כי קולך ערב
ומראיך נאוה

Let me see your face!
Let me hear your voice!
Your voice would content me
You are a vision of beauty . . .

What will she do? We want her to speak, to accept him, to come down.
This snatch of romance is short-lived and unsuccessful. Dark shadows gather and break in. They are interrupted by a terse handful of words. These words pierce the moonlight, dissipate the scent of night-flowers and stop

Earthing the Cosmic Queen

the mouths of nightingales. The outside world, has burst in and they are disrupted: (2:15) . . . *Catch the jackals / Vinespoilers!* It seems likely that these words carry an echo of those spoken by the angry sons of chapter 1.[48]

With desperate speed the poet sends the reader outwards, the *Shulamith* voices her hope: *I AM for my lover / and my lover is for me / he feasts in lotus-fields . . .*

Song 2:17

There is no recourse it seems for the heroine and she soon begs her hero to escape alone at the end of this linear development.

עד שיפוח היום

ונסו הצללים

סב דמה-לך דודי

לצבי או לעפר האילים

על-הרי בתר

Until breathes the day
And [our dark] shadows vanquished
Resemble a gazelle or young stag
On mountains of promise[49]

Song 4:3

ומדברך נאוה

Your voice is beauty!

The *Shulamith* and her hero do not speak together in chapter 3; they are separated from each other by the language of the discourse. However, in chapter 4 of the Song, the poet reiterates part of the former entreaty and

---

48. The concept of "patriarchy" as an antagonist is discussed in the section, "Brothers."

49. *Beter* is the Hebrew word used at the end of the line (2:17) and occurs only in one other verse in scripture. *Beter* is used in Genesis with respect to the Abraham's sacrificial division of animals (Gen 15:10). The context of Gen 15:10, however, is that of the most serious of covenants (which I have demonstrated through the word "promise"). I believe the author is using this mountain name implicitly referring to their vow to each other.

thus reunites these two. The Blochs' translation capitalizes on this with, *How I listen for your voice!*[50] While they may exercise too much license here, in my analysis, I also recognize it as the poet's brief but pointed reflection on an earlier idea. Speech is a key manifestation of the lovers' desire. This focus on voice/speech points to the sharing of minds as well as bodies, marking a clear and important distinction from "alien amatory literature"[51] of the same period, which more often focuses on the exhilaration of sexual activity alone.[52]

This argument strengthens by the repetition of the *until-day-breathes* refrain, 4 lines from this (4:6). This shows a clear connection in the mind of the poet with the earlier text of 2:13–17. This time the poet puts these words in the mouth of the hero. This accentuates the connectedness of the couple who seem to learn from each other; sharing their bodies and words and thoughts. Their intimacy seems more than skin deep. It seems elemental.

Song 4:8

אתי מלבנון כלה אתי מלבנון תבואי

תשורי מרוש אמוה מרוש שניר וחרמון

> Descend to me from the white mount
> My bride
> From this snow-clad mountain top come down
> Look down from the peak of Amarna
> From the summits of Senir and Hermon
> From the mountain caves of lions
> From the leopards' alpine habitat

This prose again lies at level 1 of the discourse analysis because it is a recursion to a former entreaty, particularly 2:10. For the second time the lover calls to the heroine to come down and come away. The sense of the heroine being in a loft above her hero is strong, and thus most optimally relates to the "balcony" scene of the star-crossed lovers in Song 2:8–17. The poet continues to explore this important scenario and develops it further in subsequent lines.

---

50. Bloch and Bloch, *The Song of Songs*, 73.
51. Wendland, "Seeking the Path," 25.
52. Fox, *The Song of Songs*, xxvii.

Earthing the Cosmic Queen

Song 5:1b

Song 5:1b is a significant development on the platform of entreaty. It is akin to those of the lovers but this time perhaps made by the hero to his companions.

אכלו רעים שתו ושכרו דודים

> . . . Feast comrades and drink
> Drink deeply lovers . . .

Even as early as the first real verse in the Song this prose reflects the association of kisses with wine, giving the participants that same heady feeling as though they were being gently and slowly intoxicated.

The poet is careful to employ ambiguity here. Is it the male companions of the hero addressed here, the shepherds of chapter 1, or is it you and me? Here is yet another one of those points where the poet skillfully and persuasively draws the audience. She persuades us to befriend the pair, to look upon them kindly and support their love; to see beauty in it.

Song 6:5

הסבי עיניך מנגדי שהם הרהיבני

> Turn your eyes away from me
> They overwhelm me!

The poet interrupts the erotic tension of the *wasf* for the heroine with this dramatic entreaty from her hero. This entreaty to cease looking represents the peak of the panegyric. It creates the mood of excess, that of thresholds overstepped and limits passed.[53] The dramatic tension purposefully developed by the poet also introduces the pain of love, even while in the hero's presence. The height of emotional desire and angst is beautifully expressed.

There is a pause from entreaty after this emotional peak and the poet does not return to level 1 of the discourse until the final chapter (8:6) where the *Shulamith* now moves forward from entreaty to unequivocal demand.

---

53. Pecknold uses this expression similarly in Pecknold, "The Readable City," 516–20.

Peshat: A Discourse Analysis

Song 8:6

The poet has her resound:

> שימני כחותם על-לבך כחותם על-זרועך
> כי-עזה כמות אהבה קשה כשאול קנאה
> רשפיה רשפי אש שלהבתיה

> Bare me as a seal upon your heart
> A seal upon your arm
> For love is as vehement as death
> Its passion as relentless as Sheol
> A radiating, flaming fire
> Oceans cannot overwhelm love
> Surging rivers cannot quench it . . .

Will the *Shulamith* finally find union with her lover? The Song continues at this point demonstrating that even *Shlomo* the king, cannot afford this rare treasure of love.

With such a declaration, the logical ending for the Song is a great consummation of the two lovers. But at this near end of the Song, instead of the absolute fulfilment we yearn for vicariously with the *Shulamith*, the poet twists us, twists our expectations and brings us back to the beginning with the final pair of triplets.

Song 8:13–14

The first takes us back to the entreaty to the lover's companions in 5:1 even though it is addressed to the heroine "who dwells" in the garden. *Friends listen for your voice / Let me hear it!* The poet asks the reader to join in solidarity with the lovers.

> היושבת בגנים
> חברים מקשיבים לקולך
> השמיעיני

> [Woman] living in gardens
> Our comrades listen for your voice
> Let me hear it . . .

Earthing the Cosmic Queen

But to our distress the poet brings us back to level 1 with the final line, an entreaty from the heroine to her hero to again "flee." This is the third time the heroine has used the same imagery for her lover, *gazelle, young stag*, and the second time she has begged him to flee. He too twice called her in chapter 2: *rise and go out*.

ברח דודי

ודמה-לך לצבי או לעפר האילים

על הרי בשמים

> Flee my lover
> And resemble a gazelle or young stag
> On balsam-covered mountains

It is a frustrating end to the scroll. The poet has persuaded her readers to invest in the couple, and we now long for their happiness and communion. At the very end of the Song, the poet beguiles us with the prospect of the heroine "in the garden," the place of culmination and fulfilment, but the couple is not even now together. She is there alone—but where is he? The *Shulamith*'s last words are for him to *run like a gazelle*. While the destination [*harei besamim*] may be a portent of romance [hills of balsam], the implication may be rather bittersweet. The reader expects, after such a build-up, an entreaty like, "run to me!", or better, "you and I don't have to run anymore, we're in our garden and we won't ever come out!" The intimacy of the second person is absent. The lovers are separated, and the poetic metaphor lets the hero trail away. We are left in a discomforting emotional void.[54] As Walsh would argue, we are left only with desire.[55]

The volitional mood used by the poet creates a strong sense of will and anticipation throughout the Song. This volitional mood gives the Song its potency and yet because of the jussives sporadically appearing throughout the discourse, the reader is never quite sure if these entreaties are fulfilled or whether the desires that they portray are satisfied. Jussives

---

54. Jonah is a wisdom scroll with a similarly unsatisfying ending.
55. Walsh, *Exquisite Desire*, 168.

represent the personal desires of one speaker towards another. We are left in suspense. The volitional mood also provides a loose structure to the Song. Often these volitional phrases repeat as refrains or repeat in part. They act as a platform to which the poet sporadically returns. The volitional phrases also maintain momentum and movement in the Song of Songs. The refrains of "descend" or "flee" or "rise up," give the Song the sense of multidimensional movement; geographically, topographically, and also across time. The change in scenes and scenarios also lend to this sense of ubiquity. It transcends. Volitionals such as "Let me hear you," "Let me see you," add to the sense of urgency in the Song. This urgency is often a kind of erotic tension, that of passion anticipated yet unfulfilled, but also sometimes the urgency of that is tainted by fear or sense of danger, requiring escape; running from danger and from death.

The Wasf

The second site or locale explored by the poet I have termed, as have others,[56] the *wasf* (level 2 on the discourse analysis). I include with the *wasf* that are 6 lines or more, the less developed snatches of descriptive prose that often begin with pronouns, "You are," "He is," as well as possessive adjectives, *My . . . is . . . Your . . . is . . .* which have particular power in creating and cementing connections between players and reader.[57]

As Pope notes, this genre of poetry or song is common in the Middle East.[58] The term *wasf* is Arabic meaning praise or virtue. According to Pope while *wasf* describing the beauty of women are common, those of the male are less common.[59] Similar *wasf* occur in *A Thousand and One Arabian Nights*.[60]

Fox's book *The Song of Songs and the Ancient Egyptian Love Songs* compares the Egyptian love songs and the Hebrew Song. The *wasf* of the

---

56. Falk, for example. Falk, *Song of Songs*, 80–87.

57. Not all the *"I am/You are" wasf* fragments are considered in this section. Some sit in the nexus between several other locales in the poem and will be considered there.

58. Pope, *Song of Songs*, 67.

59. Ibid.

60. Desire as a subject for songs and stories is common in the Middle East, *'ishq* is the Arabic word that means passionate desire. It is understood that the passionate love of another human has a spiritual dimension, i.e., an experience of the divine.

Song of Songs have such strong connections in style with the love poetry of Egypt, Fox categorizes its genre as Egyptian rather than Canaanite.[61]

Fox recounts that Egyptian love songs were found often in the tombs of the Pharaohs. They are short sets of songs for the simple reason that they were often painted with fine brushes on small pieces of ivory, but others appear on papyrus or other artefacts such as vases, like *The Cairo Love Songs*.[62]

The following Egyptian song that Fox calls "The Stroll" appears in the 20th dynasty papyrus found in Thebes (*P. Chester Beatty 1*).[63] "The Stroll" shows clear stylistic connections to parts of the Song such as the following *wasf* from chapter 4. This poetry consists of a series of descriptors that usually are applied to the heroine. The *wasf* begins with an epithet to her head, then descends.

Table 1: Comparison of Egyptian *wasf* "The Stroll" and Song 4:1–5

Egyptian wasf, "*The Stroll*"	Song 4:1–5
One alone is my sister / having no peer / more gracious than all other women / Behold her like Sothis rising, at the beginning of a good year / shining, precious, white of skin / lovely of eyes when gazing / sweet her lips speaking, no excess of words . . . / long of neck, white of breast / her arms surpass gold, her fingers like lotus / her full hips, her narrow waist / her thighs. . . .	So beautiful, my darling friend / so exquisite / your eyes are doves hidden in the tendrils of your hair / this hair like a flock of capering goats descending Gilead / teeth a flock of clipped ewes, ascending white and washed from the pond / two lambs to each and not one bereaved / a crimson thread to your lips / your voice is beauty. . . .

The *wasf* is a genre used throughout the Song by the poet. The characters are portrayed expressing their fascination for the other. Its impact on the reader is one of emotional investment. When I read I begin to fill out the two main characters in my imagination, personalizing them—their desires, their values, their hair color, their gods. I begin to *know* them. This development of the character grows the reader's sympathy and empathy.

---

61. Fox, *The Song of Songs*, 7.
62. Ibid., 29.
63. Ibid., 57.

Peshat: A Discourse Analysis

Song 1:3

The first *You are . . .* prose is found immediately following the first entreaty, *Let him kiss me . . .* The two connect with the repetition of the word *tovim*. An eclectic, the poet begins first with the rare part-*wasf* of the hero.

לריח שמניך טובים

שמן תורק שמך

To breathe your fragrant oils is wondrous
[Even] your name is [like] oil poured out

The couplet concludes with a gaze outwards to a new locale: *therefore, all the girls adore you . . .* , an introduction of competitors.

Song 1:9–11

לססתי ברכבי פרעה

דמיתיך רעיתי:

In this *wasf the* hero compares the heroine to one of the beautiful mares seen pulling royal Egyptian chariots: *As a mare among Pharaoh's chariot steeds / my darling friend / you excite me . . .*

This image of an equine woman is not grotesque as scholars like Fiona Black suggest.[64] The sorts of horses that belong in the stables of the wealthy in the ANE are the Ferraris and Lamborghinis of the contemporary world. She is by implication smooth, elegant, shapely, graceful, exotic, and high maintenance (!!). This is correct for any interpretation but note a single lovely mare among the virile stallions of Pharoah's chariots would create chaos. The poet has the hero reflecting on these elegant attributes and hints at the devastating, animalistic qualities these attributes bring out in his inner "stallion."[65]

---

64. Black, "Beauty or the Beast?," 303–23.
65. Hebrew and Canaanite men are occasionally likened to rutting stallions in the Hebrew Bible. One such example is Jer 5:8 and an even more graphic example of the "stallion-like" lust of people of the land occurs in Ezek 23:20.

Earthing the Cosmic Queen

נאוו לחייך בתרים
צוארך בחרוזים:
תורי זהב נעשה-לך
עם נקדות הכסף

> Beautiful cheekbones
> Circlets [at your ears] ornament them
> Your neck, with strung beads
> [A necklace] a circlet of gold embossed with silver
> We will make for you . . .

In the poet's mind is the connection between the ornamented bridle and reins of the sleek and elegant horses carrying wealthy Egyptians, and the ornaments perhaps of a less extravagant kind worn by the heroine. She deserves, the poet believes, to be better adorned than those mares. The poet has the hero wish that he could make the heroine a necklace with flashing gold and silver. He imagines how she would appear, bridled with his jewelry. This could be the thrill of the hero taking possession, the exhilaration of reigning in this high spirited, head strong woman.

Song 4:1

In the first comprehensive *wasf* the poet has the hero speak as if directly to the heroine. This takes the form of the generic *wasf*. It starts with a description of the *Shulamith's* eyes.

הנך יפה רעיתי הנך יפה

The man overwhelmed exclaims: *So beautiful / Darling friend/ So beautiful*. He imagines her eyes and hair and teeth, her eyes are full of erotic warmth *like doves*, her hair dishevelled—tangled tendrils—perhaps pulled loose from her braids by their embraces and passionate lovemaking. Her mouth is open, laughing perhaps and her white teeth are glimpsed [*sinaeq caeder hakzuvot*]. Her long hair is tumbling down, soft and flowing, like the image of goats as they run together as a herd, zigzagging, leaping and gambolling, past the rocky outcrops. In the distance they appear to flow.

Peshat: A Discourse Analysis

עיניך יונים מבעד לצמתך

שערך כעדר העזים

שגלשו מהר גלעד

> Your eyes are doves
> Hidden in the tendrils of your hair
> [This] hair like a flock of [capering] goats descending Gilead
> Teeth, A flock of clipped ewes
> Ascending white and washed from the pond
> Two lambs to each
> None bereaved

The Midrash supports the notion that women of the time used to braid their hair. The rows of goats at dawn appear like the braids of her hair: the thin lines of skin between rows of thick braids.[66] This part of the *wasf* repeats again in chapter 6.

Song 4:3

At the midpoint of this *wasf* the poet briefly returns to an earlier site of voice rather than simply objects of visual beauty, as described in the section above. The Song evokes auditory as well as visual beauty, along with scent, such as the beauty of an aroma. It is a deftly cultivated synesthaesia of beauty. She writes:

כחוט השני שפתתיך

ומדברך נאוה

> ... A crimson ribbon your lips
> Your voice fills me with content ...

The hero continues:

כפלח הרימון רקתך

מבעד לצמתך

> Like a rounded [rose-pink] pomegranate fruit
> Your [blushing] cheek
> Behind the tendrils of your hair

---

66. Lehrman, "The Song of Songs," 13.

Earthing the Cosmic Queen

This is the second of three times in the Song when the hero alludes to the *Shulamith*'s dishevelled hair. The poet's intent with this image seems to emphasize delightful abandon. This time strands of hair are resting across her cheek. Her cheek is flushed the rich, dusky pink color of pomegranate.

Song 4:4

The hero's gaze continues its journey down and he finds her neck. It is a tower [*c'migdal daveed / zuareq benui l'talpiot*] strung with shields. Two types of shields: *magaen* and *shiltim*. Both types of shields could be decorative and hung in palaces.

כמיגדל דויד

צוארך בנוי לתדפיות

אלף המגן תלוי עליו

כל שלתי הגברים

[The lithe lines of] your neck
A tower of David
A stonework turret
Strung with a thousand [golden] shields [*magaen*]
[*Shiltim*] round-shields of warriors . . .

"Long, lithe lines" the Message Bible reads and I would concur with the dynamic translation there.[67] Stately and tall, with the silhouette of a Sudanese beauty. She is stunning and exotic with a long, lithe neck. She is queenly, regal with inherent dignity.

שני שדיך כשני עפרים

תאומי צביה

הרעים בשושנים

And of course, as the hero might, when his gaze reaches her breasts he waxes lyrical: *your breasts like two fawns / twins of a gazelle / grazing in a lotus-field*. Skilfully and discreetly the poet interjects and moves dramatically back to entreaty. The entreaty is also a refrain that echoes the heroine's plea of the end of chapter 2 but now spoken by the hero.

67. Song 4:4 in Peterson, *The Message*.

Song 4:7

Almost immediately, the poet returns to the *wasf* and quickly concludes the sequence with:

כלך יפה רעיתי ומום אין בך

> You are beauty, my friend
> Nothing but perfection . . .[68]

The next verse moves into an entreaty but with a difference. This magnificent queen of a woman, a goddess of a woman, is implored to come down from the peaks of the mountains. Alternatively, this is how she may seem only to her hero alone, caught up in his passion, and we vicariously see her through his gaze. The emphasis on descent relates to the chapter 2 "balcony" scene.

Song 4:9–11

The poet has her hero's words pour out in a rush. He reveals his angst and yearning via a quasi-*wasf*, which draws upon his recounting of her body earlier in Song 4:1–7. Surprisingly he links this *wasf* with the earlier one (Song 1:10) where he pictured her as a beautiful filly and the way her necklace lay against her throat, like the flashing metal bridle on a mare's smooth, silky neck at the royal stables.

לבבתני אחתי כלה

לבבתני באחר מעיניך באחר ענק מצורוניך

> My heart is ecstatic, my sister, my bride
> You quickened me with a fleeting look
> With a flash of a link on your necklace . . .

Is the hero still glimpsing up at the *Shulamith*'s lattice window?

---

68. Marcia Falk and Ariel and Chana Bloch use *my perfect one* in their translation which is ideal. As they did, I find the construction in English of "there is no blemish in you" bulky. The Hebrew is considerably more efficient. I am indebted to these two translations here. Poem 15 from Falk, *The Song of Songs*, and, Bloch and Bloch, *The Song of Songs*, 173.

Earthing the Cosmic Queen

מה-יפו דדיך אחתי כלה
מה-טבו דדיך מיין
וריח שמניך מכל-בשמים

The hero continues with a rhythmic series of comparatives that rise to a superlative:

> How beautiful your love is
> My sister, my bride!
> How much better is your love, than wine
> And a breath of your fragrant oils
> Is the best of all the balsam....

The imagery in this line also plays again on words spoken in the outset of chapter 1 (concerning oils and wine). At the structural level, six words on either side revolve around the seventh word, and central, *tov* or, "good." This is a cue to a deeper message while on the surface the prose simply builds to a superlative. The structure draws the reader back towards a vortex.

Recurrent here is the Hebrew word *reyach*, which has the connotation of breath or breathing and of course by extension, spirit. The hero uses words here that are applicable to ecstatic experience while also having a range of other meanings. But, several of these words collectively may indicate the same extension, or invitation to the divine: *livavtiniy*, raising of the consciousness, transcendent wisdom, awakening cognitively, and, *titofnah* in the following stich which may be understood as inspiring, or prophesying.

נפת תטפנה שפתותיך כלה
דבש וחלב תחת לשונך
וריח שלמתיך כריח לבנון:

> Honeyed words from your lips inspire me
> Bride
> Honey and milk flow in your voice...
> And in your clothes I breathe a scent
> Like that of Lebanon

The poet is very concerned to continue to invoke the voice of the *Shulamith* and we see here a recursion. It is as if the voice of the *Shulamith* brings her hero to wholeness or higher consciousness (humanizes, quickens, animates, brings to life, like the breath of God in Genesis 1). The word *reyach* scent, breeze, spirit, wind occurs three times in this short sequence. It is of interest that the poet routinely interrupts these *wasf* with the intangible idea of voice or speech, and breath.[69] Here again we see a movement back to the site of the entreaties and the themes there which the poet explores. The poet seems to want to develop the value of the voice and the words of both lovers. The intimacy between the lovers seems to be, while fully embracing physical beauty and biological attraction, one that is a deep meeting of minds, a mythical, total union. This deep expression of passion is creative and constructive. The divine, rather than ritual, is experienced in this passionate love.

Song 5:10–16

There is a long deviation between the part-*wasf* of chapter 4 and the next *wasf* set. The poet's gaze moves outwards to the furthest locale with a transient exploration of "the garden." Slowly after this almost-climax she descends through another "losing/finding" sequence, where the *Shulamith* framed by desperation begins to work through each of her hero's features, as if to recount each part will reconstruct him and make him appear, or recounting each part of him lest the precious memory of him begins to fade. Hence we have here the first of only two full *wasf* and it is of the hero (as we have mentioned earlier, *wasf* with a man as the object is rare in comparative literature) in the Song of Songs.[70]

Her hero is radiant and flushed with life.[71] He is a banner; a prince among men.[72] His head shines with purest gold. His thick, curled mane of hair is raven-black [*orev*].

דודי צח ואדום דגול מרבבה

ראשו כתם פז

קווצותיו תלתלים שחרות כעורב:

---

69. The rich descriptive discourse in the Song is imaginative and colorful. The lovers create their own paradise. This may mimic the divine, creative speech that created the world in Genesis when God pronounced, *Y'hi ohr* (Gen 1:3). This concordance with Genesis is explored in *Remez*.

70. Pope, *Song of Songs*, 56.

71. Note Gen 49:12 where Judah's "messiah" is ". . . red with wine, and his teeth white with milk."

72. In Isaiah, the *messiah*, "Root of Jesse," is a banner (Isa 11:10).

My love is dazzling white and wine-red
He stands like a banner in a myriad
His head shines with pure gold
His thick mane is raven-black . . .

Her hero's eyes like her own are hot with emotion; like doves by a bubbling brook. They are, inconceivably, bathed in milk—apparently white, clear, well, and pure. His eyes are full, intense and these are the gates to his *nefesh*, the home of his *neshamah*.

עיניו כיונים על-אפיקי מים

רחצות בחלב ישבות על-מלאת

His eyes impassioned doves
Pure, clear, milk-white
He dwells in their fullness . . .

Myrrh is a fragrant tree resin that is often used at burials as it is pungent rather than fragrant and has a purifying quality.

לחיו כערוגת הבשם מגדלות מרקחים

שפתותיו שושנים נטפות מור עבר

His cheeks are terraces of balsam
Cone-towers of aromatic spice
[From] his lips [knowing words] flow like myrrh
From a lotus

Envisioned here, this pungent oil is dripping from the hero's lips, not sprinkled or in a sachet or burned. Myrrh is very bitter to taste and presumably the *Shulamith* tastes his mouth when they kiss. Does the poet imply through this innuendo that the hero's words are strong, hard to hear or cleansing, cathartic, awakening?[73] Myrrh is used elsewhere in the Hebrew bible as a kind of toilette.[74] The structure of the *wasf* distances the lovers.

---

73. Again, this emphasis on voice is linked to *Eden*. The couple's voices and words are a focal point; like God's creative speech. These two create their own paradise through words.

74. In Prov 7:17 it is used to perfume a bed prior to an adulterous event. In Esther 2:12 it is an essential part of a rigorous six month cosmetic toilette for concubines chosen for the King's harem. It is amongst the oils and spices comissioned for the *Mishkan*, Exod 30, and to perfume women's court attire in Ps 45. Walsh goes into some detail regarding the hygiene habits and necessities in Ancient Israel, where perfumes and oils like myrrh

Peshat: A Discourse Analysis

He becomes her object. From this vantage point his myrrh-scented mouth is breathed, not tasted.

ידיו גלילי זהב ממלאים בתרשיש

מעיו עשת שן מעלפת ספירים

His hands are wheels of gold
Filled in with sea-green[75] chrysoprase [tarshish-stone][76]
The seat of his manhood[77] carved ivory
Encrusted with lapis lazuli . . .

There is a movement in this part of the Song away from a near and earthy description of the hero towards a more transcendent and intangible imagining of him. The poet has the hero becoming awe-inspiring, like a vision of a god-King. The lapis lazuli, in comparative Egyptian sculpture, represents the "ocean of the sky," the home of the gods.[78] This imagery finds its source in the stone gods of the type transported via palanquin or gurney through cities in the ANE and established in temples.[79] Worshippers anoint such statues with precious oils, and burn fragrant incense at their feet. The imagery of this divine-man continues.

---

were even more significant to maintain an attractive scent because of the scarcity of water for washing. Walsh, *Exquisite Desire*, 60.

75. All three targums on Exod 28:20 describe the stone as "the color of the sea" according to John Gill (1690–1771), who reflects on this in his exposition of Song 5:14, Gill, *Exposition on the Old Testament*.

76. An unidentified stone that some scholars believe is a semi-precious gem found in Tarshish, which could be olivine, chrysolite, jasper, beryl, even emerald. Some understand a particular kind of opaque quartz was mined in Tarshish and upon heating becomes translucent yellow-brown. Chrysoprase is a kind of quartz that is a beautiful sea-green color and I have chosen this with respect to the Targum.

77. The Hebrew word *ma'eh* means: bowels, belly, abdomen, womb, loins. In almost all cases in scripture when it concerns a man it is implying his procreative organs (the place where his seed is stored, the house of future generations). With this in mind I have used "seat of his manhood" to better capture the connotation. The root term *ma'eh* can also refer to the emotions of particularly sympathy.

78. Keel, *The Song of Songs*, 202.

79. Wendland and Keel both recognize the source of this imagery as the idols of the day. Wendland, "Seeking the Path," 17, and Keel, *The Song of Songs*, 202–3. The significance of the stone god is explored in the final chapter *Remez-Derasha*.

Earthing the Cosmic Queen

שוקיו עמודי שש מיסדים על-אדני-פז
מראהו כלבנון בחור כארזים

> His thighs alabaster pillars
> His calves [establish themselves on] pedestals of fine gold
> He appears like the white mountain [*Lebanon*]
> [His aspect] towering cedars . . .

The *wasf* ends with a reference to the voice/mouth/speech of the hero. His speaking removes all bitter and burdensome things and shifts them to the periphery. Once more we hear the refrain of avowal to the daughters of Jerusalem.

חכו ממתקים וכלו מחמדים
זה דודי וזה רעי בנות ירושלם

> His speech [mouth] is sweet
> And all delight
> This is my love
> And this is my friend
> Daughters of Jerusalem

The heroine brings us gently back down from the "ocean of the sky" to earth. "How great is he?" they had asked, "As great as the sons of gods!" she seems to reply. Her hero is great as a pharaoh, a king, a living god.

Song 6:4–7

In this *wasf* the hero once again begins to recount the features of his *Shulamith*. She is beautiful and her beauty is potent. To him she has the grandeur of the great cities like Tirzah and Jerusalem. In fact, she is breathtaking in her beauty, as if he was looking upon a legion of warriors carrying their bright flags and banners.

יפה את רעיתי כתרצה
נאוה כירושלם אימה כנדגלות
הסבי עיניך מנגדי שהם הרהיבני

> Beautiful are you, my friend
> Like Tirzah
> Enchanting as Jerusalem

Peshat: A Discourse Analysis

> Breath-taking as a myriad of banners
> Look away from me
> Your eyes overwhelm me!

Her beauty confuses, overwhelms and terrifies. Her gaze burns. He entreats her to *turn your eyes away from me*. He cannot bear her gaze.

At this point the poet's *wasf* takes a more formal structure beginning with her hair. This *wasf* is at once familiar and is indeed adapted and developed from another *wasf* in chapter 4. In contrast to the introduction of this particular *wasf* the poet changes tack and the hero is no longer "awestruck" but returns to more delicate and quaint metaphors such as ones based on gentle agricultural imagery in order to describe her in intimate terms.

שערך כעדר העזים שגלשו מן-הגלעד
שניך כעדר הרחלים שעלו מן-הרחצה
שכלם מתאימות ושכלה אין בהם:
כפלח הרמון רקתך מבעד לצמתך:

> [Your] hair is like a flock of goats descend Gilead
> [Your] teeth are like a flock of clipped ewes
> Ascending white and washed from the pond
> Two lambs to each and none bereaved
> Like rounded [rose-pink] pomegranate your cheek
> Behind the tendrils of your hair . . .

The *wasf* of chapter 6 concentrates on the eyes, hair, teeth and temple of the heroine. It goes no further. The *wasf* genre is left behind as the poet's gaze moves significantly into locale of *the garden*.

Song 7:1b–6

מה-יפו פעמיך בנעלים בת-נדיב

The *wasf* that begins chapter 7 is an inclusio encased by two references to royalty. The first describes the *Shulamith* as the daughter of an aristocrat while the last reference describes the "king," her lover, caught in the tendrils of her hair.

But in chapter 7 the poet creates a reverse *wasf* that moves from the feet of the heroine back up towards her head. Chapter 6 has ended with an entreaty from a crowd to dance. It is not clear whether these are friends or outsiders. The *wasf* of chapter 7 seems like a continuation of the dance, but this time a single male voice speaks and it seems to be her hero though this is not made clear (apart from the precedent of interaction already established in the Song).

חמוקי ירכיך כמו חלאים מעשה ידי אמן:

Somewhere in the crowd her princely lover seems to be watching and as he begins to describe her dance we move from public space to private space. He begins at her feet distantly: *How beautiful are your steps [even] in sandals / prince's daughter . . .*

But urgently the hero's gaze moves to focus on her "seat of generation" a mirrored response to the masculine *wasf* of chapter 5.

שררך אגן הסהר אל-יחסר המזג

> The joints of your thighs are jewelled
> The handiwork of an artisan
> Your "navel"[80] is like a hammered basin[81]
> That mulled wine never ebbs . . .

Once again the imagery finds its source in sacred sculpture of the ANE. A sculptor has worked this stone goddess with passionate and ornate detail; an eye for beauty.

בתנך ערמת חטים סוגה בשושנים

> Your belly / a dome of wheat / encircled by lotus

In nature ponds and lakes are encircled by water-lotus. In the evening the pond reflects the moonlight (probably the source of the hammered basin imagery above).

The poet has left behind the imagery of sacred sculpture and moves into the sanctity of the natural world with mention of wild gazelle.

שני שדיך כשני עפרים תאמי צביה

> Your breasts like two fawns / twins of a gazelle . . .

---

80. The progression of the *wasf* seems to indicate that "navel" is indeed a euphemism.
81. As if it was the moon, glistening in the night sky . . .

Peshat: A Discourse Analysis

The poet adjusts her gaze again. She introduces the imagery of architecture to paint with words the statuesque beauty and potency or strength of the heroine. Awe stirs with reference to sacred mountains, and also purity (the "whiteness") of her skin is embodied in the reference to *Lebanon*, the white, snow-clad mountain.

צוארך כמגדל השן

עיניך ברכות בחשבון על-שער בת-רבים

אפך כמגדל הלבנון צופה פני דמשק

רושך עליך ככרמל ודלת ראשך כארגמן

מלך אסור ברהטים:

    The lithe lines of your neck like an ivory tower
    Your eyes pools of Heshbon
    By the gates of Bat-Rabim[82]
    Your nose like the summit of Lebanon
    [its snow-clad] face overlooking Damascus
    Your head ascends like Carmel
    Magenta threads fixed in your hair
    Tendrils[83] of hair capture a king

This woman, even in the plainest sandals, is empowered through the poet's expansive scope in metaphor. In a social world where women are vulnerable (i.e., 5:7), the most powerful man in the kingdom is captivated by her. The *wasf* ends with a brief line that moves the gaze away from the intensity that built through the *wasf*, becoming less direct though still voluptuous:

מה-יפת ומה-נעמת אהבה בתענוגים

    How beautiful
    And how enchanting
    Daughter of ecstasy!

---

82. Lit. "daugther of great ones."
83. This evokes Abraham and Isaac in Gen 22:13 where the thicket by the altar entrapped a ram. Some translations have "thicket" for *rahtim*. I have "tendrils" which better supports the notion of woman's hair yet maintains the "disheveled" quality that *rahtim* connotes (rather than bushy).

Earthing the Cosmic Queen

The poet in the *wasf* prose draws the consenting reader to invest emotionally in the protagonists by developing them visually and descriptively. These connections or sensations of familiarity and knowing facilitate empathy. By the end of the Song we know the passion of the lovers, especially the passion of the heroine, and place high value on it. To produce a dramatic tension, the poet may have intended the *wasf* to be envisioned as soliloquies by the two protagonists even though some dreamy interjection appears. These moments of discourse with the other evoke a sense of connection and an element of conversation between the lovers. On the other hand these soliloquies could be performed by the heroine alone and/or the party of young women, performing by memory or in anticipation of the hero's words as in role-play.[84]

Many of the *wasf* consist of complementing pairs, characteristic of the Hebrew poetic formula. An initial metaphor or simile is complemented and accentuated by a second adverbial or adjectival phrase.[85] Metaphors are transformed into hyperboles, overflowing with excess: *his hands are wheels of gold / filled in with tarshish-stone*. The *wasf* use hyperbole and dramatic contrast to heighten the romantic tension in the Song. Some of the *wasf* prose is erotic, almost graphic. The poet unapologetically employs startling innuendo, such that when the meaning is glimpsed, the gentle reader experiences a shock of exposure.

The imagery used in the *wasf* moves from natural, to agricultural, to military/royalty. The imagery used from these spheres in the poet's society accentuates various qualities of the couple. The poet characterizes the heroine, surprisingly even more so than the hero, as strong, brave and stoic as well as sweet, lovely, soft and graceful.

---

84. This sort of play-acting by women does occur in betrothal ceremonies in some modern agrarian societies. Women gather and sing songs for the *kallah* (bride) and these songs may involve role–playing the parts of father and brothers. The expressive singing (the Song of the "unknown lover") in the henna ritual of Sephardi brides in Yemen is also notable, Sharaby, "The Bride's Henna Ritual," 22–23.

85. Wendland describes this feature of Hebrew poetry in detail in Wendland, "Seeking the Path," 18.

Daughters

The daughters [*banot*] are an essential and significant group in the Song and perhaps first recognized by the poet in the first few lines *all the young women want you* (1:3b). In this vignette, the reference seems to be ephemeral and not a direct concern for the poet, although groups of women appear throughout. The daughters, here, are portrayed then dismissed as "competitors," serving to heighten the desirability of the hero.

In an agrarian culture characterized by kinship groups, the daughters, *banot*, are featured appropriately as pubescent or prepubescent unmarried girls. They are responsible to their fathers and brothers or uncles.[86] For a good portion of the Song, these daughters feature as an audience or perhaps even *the* primary audience for *Shulamith's* dream of love.

The *banot Yerushalayim* [daughters of Jerusalem] are not insiders though the heroine confides in them and shares the same set of societal constraints as they do. In some passages the daughters are outsiders not truly knowing or caring for the heroine's plight. Some parts of the Song have the daughters acting in a supportive role, and some of the references to them are instructive. Occasionally the heroine seems to despair about their lack of understanding. Some of the heroine's reminiscences seem to be addressed to the daughters though often these addresses move inwards into soliloquy. Movement is one of the great constants of the Song.

The heroine four times entreats the daughters to make an oath to her (a "seven") and three of these entreaties ask *not to awaken love*.[87] This is as if young women should suppress their fledgling passions. This is ironic because the young woman, the *Shulamith*, seems to do the very opposite. However the poet creates a further sequence (3:11) when the heroine entreats the daughters (this time daughters of Zion) to come out. In that instance, the daughters are also requested to "gaze upon" *Shlomo* or perhaps *Shlomo's* mother. This is as if to rouse and awaken higher consciousness through sight.

Seven times the poet has the daughters speak as a group. Their contribution to the Song comes in the form of questions. Three of the questions are asked about the heroine: "Who is that rising?" and the other four frame the *wasf* of the god-like hero in chapter 5.

---

86. Meyers, *Discovering Eve*, 187.

87. This is Song 2:7, 3:5, 8:4 (8:4 varies slightly) and 5:8 asks the women to vow to find the lover.

Earthing the Cosmic Queen

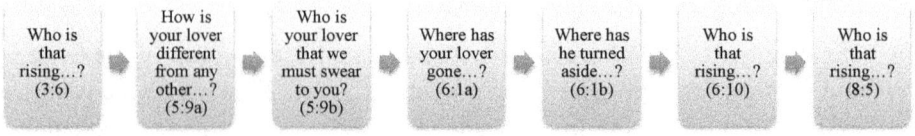

Figure 3: Questions asked by the *banot yerushalaim*

Song 1:3b

The daughters first enter the Song at the end of the first masculine *wasf* in chapter 1. You are fragrant, you are myrrh, *all the young women adore you*, the poet claims.

על-כן עלמות אהבוך

Song 1:5–6a

The poet clearly intends to introduce the young women as players in the drama. She moves to an address that has the daughters acting as confidants. It quickly becomes soliloquy that could invoke the image of the daughters listening quietly as confidants. The subject of the address is the heroine and her plight, her conflict with her brothers, who represent the powers that be in her society—powers that can constrain her love.

שחורה אני ונאוה בנות ירושלם
כאהלי קדר כיריעות שלמה
אל-תראני שאני שחרחרת
ששזפתני השמש

I am dark but I am desirable, daughters of Jerusalem / dark as the bedouin tents of Kedar, lovely as the tapestries of Solomon, says the heroine. The poet has this *Shulamith* make a claim that she is worth more than how she is perhaps presently perceived by her society. In this speech the daughters seem to be included with the "outsiders" even though they are in her circle. In the heroine's next statement she reproves them: *Do not see me as black,*

Peshat: A Discourse Analysis

I have been pierced by the Sun's rays. From this point the poet's gaze moves outwards to introduce *the brothers* as the cause of her distress. She is the object of their anger.

Song 2:7, 3:5

השבעתי אתכם בנות ירושלם
בצבאות או באילות השדה אם-תעירו
ואם-תעוררו את-האהבה עד שתחפץ

> Daughters of Jerusalem
> Swear to me [completely][88]
> By the gazelles and the does in the field
> That you never rouse nor awaken love
> Until it is full . . .

Both 2:7 and 3:5 contain the same lines word for word in the original language and I consider them together here and note that the poet may have intended these lines to frame the interceding material.

In the first instance, the heroine seems caught in a waking dream, remembering or imagining a love scene that was for her a time of exquisite celebration, a time of light. Suddenly the poet has the *Shulamith* rouse from her reverie to charge her peers to guard love. Othmar Keel has *ahavah* being as skittish and fey as wild deer.[89]

In the second instance, the avowing occurs after a short, troubled quasi-narrative. This time the *Shulamith* recounts what is either a dream or symbol-rich story. In this account, the poet has her experience the dark pain of love, a painful tale of loss, and the heart-wrenching search for something that has become more valuable than anything she holds dear, even more than her own life. She risks all and goes out into the night, into the city. The adjuring of the daughters of Jerusalem now becomes a refrain that concludes the narrative but also links the dark passage to chapter 2 and its theme of the lightness of love. The heights and depths of love contrast via this clever stylistic ruse.

---

88. The notion of "seven" is involved in this vow-making. I have tried to illustrate this by adding "completely" as seven was considered as symbolic "completion" or "perfection" as was the creation on the seventh day.

89. Keel, *The Song of Songs*, 94.

Earthing the Cosmic Queen

The *Shulamith* asks her peers to swear by the deer and the gazelle in the field, never to rouse or awaken love until it is full.[90] This phrase seems to indicate something of the delicate balance of romantic, young love that requires time and the right environment to be in balance, to mature, to be *tov*. Whose love this is, is not clear in the Hebrew. It seems simultaneously to be the *Shulamith*'s love, not excluding the love of her hero if *ahavah* is considered generic.[91] But importantly the entreaty and the ambiguity allows the troth to stretch past the players in the Song towards the reader.

Song 3:6

מי זאת עלה מן-המדבר

כתימרות עשן

מקטרת מר ולבונה מכל אבקת רוכל

> Who is this? [Fem.]
> She rises from the wilderness
> Like a pillar of cloud
> Smoke of myrrh and frankincense
> All the spices of a camel-train . . .

This is the first *Mi zot* question addressed reflectively by the daughters. The first seems to locate the heroine, not in *Shlomo's* palanquin which follows in 3:11, but in the Exodus, where the cloud preceded the caravan of Israel, and closely linked, the smoke of incense dispersed in the ritual in the Temple.[92] This has a sacral function in the poet's development of the heroine. There is a divine approbation and sacredness in her desire to fulfill her love with her own *Shlomo*.[93]

---

90. Lit. "pleased" or "desires." Chana and Ariel Bloch use "ripe"; see Bloch and Bloch, *The Song of Songs*, 57.

91. *ahavah* is feminine in the Hebrew and *shetechpats* has an ambiguous female referent which could equally be interpreted as she (the *Shulamith*) or it (love).

92. See Exod 13:21; Lev 16:13.

93. Her hero, the one in whom she finds "His peace" (8:10).

Peshat: A Discourse Analysis

Song 3:11

צאנה וראינה בנות ציון
במלך שלמה בעטרה
שעטרה-לו אמו
ביום חתנתו וביום שמחת לבו

> Arise daughters of Zion
> And behold the king [of Peace]
> [See] the crown with which his mother crowned him
> On the day of his wedding
> The day of the joy of his heart

In the preceding *mittah* vignette of 3:7–10, the poet focuses on a palanquin of *Shlomo*; he made it. And the daughters of Jerusalem wrought the interior out of their love (3:10b). In this address, the poet uniquely transforms the identity of the *banot yerushalaim*. They are now the daughters of Zion. This could infer some kind of growth. The daughters of Jerusalem sometimes understand and sometimes doubt. By implication, the daughters of Zion may have *awakened*, (spiritual or otherwise), that enables them to *za'ina* and *ra'ina*, to rise up and perceive. Zion is the sacred hill of Jerusalem, the place of the temple, the place of the heart and eyes of God.[94]

Song 5:8, 9, 16b; 6:1

A second dream sequence occurs in chapter 5. It resembles the sequence of chapter 3 with the same players. This time the ending is violent. The heroine suffers abuse at the hands of the watchmen and is left with deep loss. This time the heroine's entreaty to the daughters of Jerusalem reaches a fevered pitch.

השבעתי אתכם בנות ירושלם
אם-תמצאו את-דודי מה-תגידו לו
שחולת אהבה אני

---

94. Isa 2:3, Mic 4:2. In this instance, the daughters belong to Zion rather than Jerusalem, which may point to the prophetic notion of Zion as the future perfection of Jerusalem. This sort of juxtaposition of Jerusalem and Zion is common but not consistent in Isaiah; i.e., Isa 4:5.

Earthing the Cosmic Queen

> Swear to me [completely]
> All you daughters of Jerusalem
> If you find my darling
> How you must tell him
> Tell him I am afflicted by love . . .

In this instance, the poet has the daughters respond sarcastically:

מה-דודך מדוד היפה בנשים

מה-דודך מדוד שככה השבעתנו

> What is your lover compared to another
> "Beautiful among women"
> What is your lover compared to another
> That you would ask us to swear

In this question there is an indication that the daughters were listening to other addresses. They have heard the heroine protest that even though her skin is dark with her labors, she is still desirable. They have heard her reminisce, over and over, of their meetings, his virtues, her fantasies. In reply to this question the heroine launches into the full *wasf* of her hero that virtually proclaims he is more than a man. He is a god. This is another sacred peak in the Song. She completes her *wasf* with the exultant words:

זה דודי וזה רעי בנות ירושלם

> This is my darling
> And this is my friend
> Daughters of Jerusalem . . .

The *Shulamith*'s words have affected the daughters of Jerusalem and they are now convinced that the lover is worth reconsidering her plea. Chapter 6 clearly follows on in this quasi narrative.

אנה הלך דודך היפה בנשים

אנה פנה דודך ונבקשנו עמך:

The young women have softened and ask further:

> Where has he journeyed, your lover?
> Which way has your lover turned?
> And we will search him out with you . . .

Peshat: A Discourse Analysis

At this point the narrative twists and deforms. Far from being unsure of her lover's whereabouts the *Shulamith* knows exactly where he has gone and the daughters are rebuffed and then forgotten.

Song 6:10

מי-זאת הנשקפה כמו-שחר יפה כלבנה
ברה כחמה אימה כנדגלות

Who is this? [Fem.]
She appears like the dawn
Beauty like the white moon
Searing like the sun's rays
Terrible as the myriad shining stars . . .

This is the second question of this sort spoken by the *banot Yerushalaim*. The first of their questions in Song 3:6 drew upon the iconic scene of the Mosaic desert caravan led by cloud. This second is an expansion of the first. The vision is that of the heavenly beings: the rising sun, the luminous moon, the midday sun and the stars in their constellations. She is the universe.

Song 8:4, 5a

We return to the daughters again in the final portion of the Song. Once again the same refrain is used. The daughters are beseeched to pledge their word. This time they are not asked to swear by the gazelles and the does in the fields. This request for a vow was triggered for the second time by the whispered reverie (Song 8:3): *s'molo tachat roshi v'yamini tachabkeni* or in translation, *his left hand beneath my head and his right hand embraces me*. The intimate details of their lovemaking bring about a sudden consciousness of the immediate context and a vow from the daughters of Jerusalem.

השבעתי אתכם בנות ירושלם
מה-תעירו ומה-תעררו את-האהבה
עד שתחפץ

> Swear to me [without exception][95]
> All you daughters of Jerusalem
> Never rouse nor awaken love
> until it is full

This is the third time the poet has Shulamith beseech this oath and I attempt to show through the addition of, "without exception" how the message has intensified with this repetition and also become more dramatically abrupt with the omission of phrases. This appears to signal this message as an important one, with the poet consistently attributing the lines to heroine who speaks them out to the young women of the city.

The request for the vow brings about a response in the form of a question or echo. It is not entirely clear who is asking this question but it seems the young women are the likely ones, perhaps voicing it for the reader. Perhaps the entire chorus is evoked her. We cannot help but ask too. At this point in the text we are its subject, completely invested in the outcome. It is only clear that the *Shulamith* is not the one asking, as it seems as if the poet has her in mind as the subject of it.

מי זות עלה מן-המדבר מתרפקת על-דודך

> Who is this? [Fem]
> Coming up from the wilderness
> Reclining against her lover?

This final question from the daughters again locates the heroine in the desert-wilderness, but this time united with her hero. It is perhaps the only scene where the two lovers are unmistakeably set together, witnessed by all, the whole community. This is striking in a song obsessed with love and desire. The lovers are referred to in fourth person as it were; [96] the lovers neither know nor care that they are observed. The scene is set at distance but even this mirage of their consummation engenders benevolent warmth in the reader. There is *shalom* invoked here and in response, the poet seems to pause for a moment. The scene is more robust than simple reverie. The association of the Exodus journeying in the desert is poignant. The woman ascends as if she was all of Israel, from the desert, as if into a

---

95. The addition of "without exception" represents the intensification of this chorus due to its third repetition.

96. Fourth person is characteristically speaking of someone who is not present and therefore not listening. This becomes an irony in the Song when fourth person is used of *Shlomo*. He seems oblivious in the Song to the part he plays (particularly 8:11–12).

Promised Land. This sacred journey of ascent also draws the reader into the sacred history of the Hebrews. In this consummation she communes with the Divine. So it is not by chance that now the voices of the daughters diminish as the dramatic expression of the heroine returns to the fore and reaches a crescendo.

The daughters of Jerusalem play a strategic role in the Song of Songs. Their relationship with the heroine is subordinate. She dispenses wisdom to them, but at other times must persuade them. She is rebuked by them. Their interaction with the *Shulamith* provides movement in the Song and also provides further foils from which the lovers may be perceived. The presence of the daughters as players in the drama, directly engaged by the heroine, enables the poet to facilitate the vicarious approach of her reader, who is subtly drawn in to be made wise by the *Shulamith*.

Royalty

One of the great conflicts and inconsistencies in the Song of Songs is the way that the poet uses the trope of royalty. Royalty, and the life and luxury of the elite pervades the Song to color the settings in which the lovers are imagined but figures of royalty are also purloined by the poet (8:11–12). One of the conflicting aspects of the Song is the way the poet utilizes the character, *Shlomo haMelek* (Solomon, the King). Some parts of the Song seem to laud *Shlomo* and his lifestyle, such as the superscript.

Song 1:1

שיר השירים אשר לשלמה

The Song of Songs which is *Shlomo's* seems to suggest an intimate connection between Solomon and the Song. However in the superscript it is perhaps not *Shlomo haMelek* whom we know from scripture as a profligate womanizer, but as Rashi believes a pointer to "him to whom peace belongs" and we have noted earlier how much peace, *shalom*, is a feature in the Song, (a song which is also in most of its states more in turmoil than in peace).

Song 1:4b

הביאני המלך חדריו

He has brought me, the King, into his most private place: a phrase embodying dramatic movement. Her lover, her hero becomes—*haMelek*—an awe-inspiring royal title and yet one that distances. It is exclusive. The reader is detached, excluded. This is made dramatically more so as prior to and after the phrase the use of personal pronouns is drawing the audience in: *bring me, we will run together and we will be glad,* which in my reading is the joy of the hero and heroine together, not the joy of three hundred concubines. The deeper implication seems to be *He has brought me* [that is, not you] into his most private place [a place, you, or other women, cannot come]. Perhaps reading between the lines the heroine demarcates a boundary of intimacy that onlookers and even friends/comrades cannot intrude.

Song 1:12

עד-שהמלך במסבו נרדי נתן ריחו

> As the king reclines
> On his spacious divan
> My musk-scented nard
> Its fragrance breathes

Here the poet connects us with the first use of *melek* in the chapter. In between, the Song has twisted and turned through scenes of viticulture and pastures, but this return gives coherence to the chapter and the Song thus far. The second use of the word *melek* and the context of reclining in a private suite in between these pastoral scenes leads to a slow revelation that the two lovers are not in fact in a stone palace in the city, but in a grotto formed of living trees, curtained with vines and leaves and carpeted with grass. The epiphany may also include recognition that the hero is as if a king but only to her and the heroine as if she was a queen but only to him. For everyone else involved, this is simply risky foolishness.

Peshat: A Discourse Analysis

My musk-scented nard / Its fragrance breathes: the Blochs have "wakened the night," which is a lovely, dynamic translation.[97] According to the New Bible Dictionary perfumes like nard were particularly used to anoint couches where the wealthy would recline and feast and make love (Pro 7:17).[98] It is important to sense the distance the word *haMelek* connotes here. When the heroine talks about herself the poet has her use first person which makes her tangible and provocative. *HaMelek* however is distant and intangible. Another option is that these two conflicting parts of speech hold us in a tension that mimics the frustrated desire of star-crossed lovers. The reader is distanced and lured in at the same time.

Song 3:7–11

Solomon, the King, does feature in the Song in the third or perhaps fourth person.[99] In chapter 3 close to the centre of the Song, he appears by name in three sequential interconnected yet disparate poem-vignettes.

He first appears as a character after she "comes up from the desert" with strong connotations of the Exodus, pillars of cloud, but perfumed here rather than desert-weary and faint of heart. Many readings see this first Solomon vignette as following on from the question "Who is this?" however this must be reconciled with the way "Who is this?" is repeated as a refrain two other times but clearly referring to the heroine.[100] The poet seems to make one of her distinctive breaks from the flow of the narrative. She leaves us with the image of the heroine rising from the desert and then in the same instant switches to a mirror image, an ironic foil, featuring the King.

הנה מטתו שלשלמה
ששים גברים סביב לה מגברי ישראל
כלם אחזי חרב מלמדי מלחמה

97. Bloch and Bloch, *The Song of Songs*, 53.
98. Douglas et al., "Cosmetics and Perfumery," 231.
99. See prior footnote in this section on the significance of fourth person.
100. Exum reads the *who is this* question and the following *mittah* vignette as a clever movement from distance to intimacy. The view of the *mittah* becomes ever closer. However I would like to argue that there is a juxtaposing of "things of men" and "things of women" in this sequence that may support the shift from heroine to the irony of *Shlomo*. Exum, "Seeing Solomon's Palanquin," 305.

Earthing the Cosmic Queen

איש חרבו על-ירכו מפחד בלילות

> Oh, the caravan of *Shlomo*
> Sixty warriors surround it
> [These] are the bravest in Israel
> Each of them holds a sword tried in war
> A man's sword at his thigh
> Against the fears of night

Shlomo is, in this first of three episodes, in his litter surrounded by the valiant men of Israel. The reference to *fears of the night* echoes the fear of the *Shulamith* in the beginning of the chapter as she wrestles with her dark dreams. However, this caravan is travelling in daylight and the preoccupation with night terrors seems overstated. There seems to be a dramatic contrast intended by the poet here. The woman in the earlier piece fought her night terrors without a sword. She, with no defence, goes into the night. Solomon on the other hand, insulates himself, walls himself in with a platoon of body guards, warriors. Where is his courage in comparison to *Shulamith*? The swords have made him unapproachable. His love by analogy is jaded, defensive. This woman by contrast is fearless when she loves. She gives everything.

אפריון עשה לו המלך שלמה מעצי הלבנון

עמודיו עשה כסף רפידתו זהב מרכבו ארגמן

תוכו רצוף אהבה מבנות ירושלם

> A palanquin he made himself the king, *Shlomo*
> From wood of Lebanon
> Its stands he made silver
> Its cover gold
> Its couch purple
> The interior wrought by the daughters of Jerusalem
> Out of their love

Secondly and immediately following is another snapshot of *Shlomo* as he builds another exquisite palanquin inlaid with the love of the daughters of Jerusalem.[101] The poet evokes the Ark of the Covenant in Exodus 25. There is no mention of the armed warriors here, no military presence. This

---

101. The palanquin is made of silver and purple along with wood from Lebanon which are specific items mentioned in the building of the Temple by *Shlomo* in 2 Chr 2.

Peshat: A Discourse Analysis

is the longest stich, and thereby strongly evidencing that the focus in the vignette belongs to the daughters who contributed to the building of this precious palanquin with love.

And the third—the gentle reader is transported to Solomon's wedding day, seeing it vicariously through the eyes of the daughters of Zion and his mother crowning him; an intriguing and extraordinary scene. Here the festivity seems to belong to the realm of women. The mother is in a place of authority in the ceremony. In this ceremony even the king of the nation must look to her.

צאנה וראינה בנות ציון במלך שלמה
בעטרה שעטרה-לו אמו
ביום חתנתו וביום שמחת לבו

Arise, daughters of Zion
Behold the king [of Peace]
[**See**] the crown with which his mother crowned him
On the day of his wedding
The day of the joy of his heart

The poet, in these three Solomonic vignettes, purposes to feature a strong contrast between the ways of women—characterised by *love*—and the ways of men, characterised by *war*. These social domains of men and women in Israel contrasted by the poet seem to polarise the scene into gendered realms: war/power, and, love/joy. With the Song's continuing approbation of the heroine, in all her ventures, whether the outcomes are pleasant or harsh, the poet seems to suggest that women because of their investment in love prevail in ways that the powerful and the workers of war do not.[102]

Song 6:8, 9

It is not always clear whether the poet imagines the heroine as from the noble classes. In earlier parts of the Song, she is figured as a royal bride or concubine, but in others, a shepherdess.[103] In this vignette in chapter 6, the poet's heroine is compared to royal women with the implication that even if

---

102. This will be discussed in depth in the *Remez* chapter.
103. See 1:2ff.

Earthing the Cosmic Queen

she is a commoner she is as worthy as or even better than them, in the eyes of her hero. The vignette takes form in an intricate chiasm.

ששים המה מלכות ושמנים פילגשים

ועלמות אין מספר

אחת היא יונתי

תמתי אחת היא לאמה

ברה היא ליולדתה

ראוה בנות ויאשרוה

מלכות ופילגשים ויהללוה

> There are 60 queens, and 80 of the king's women
>   And girls without number
>   She is unique my dove
>   She is perfectly unique of her mother
>   The beloved one of she who birthed her
>   Daughters saw her
> Queens blessed her, and the king's women gave praise.

Song 7:2, 8

Again in chapter 7 the poet links the heroine with royalty and this first line becomes the theme of an entire *wasf*. In this sequence the heroine may be royal or may be a peasant girl. This could be a panegyric on the part of the hero, or a literal description. The preceding vignette in chapter 6 perhaps indicates the poet is writing figuratively, and certainly the *wasf* that follows is pure hyperbole.

מה-יפו פעמיך בנעלים בת-נדיב

> How beautiful you are
> [Even] in sandals
> Prince's daughter . . .

The royal connotations in the introductory line of the *wasf* link to the closing line in the *wasf* forming an inclusio based around the poet's idealizing of the couple as royal lovers. The last line reads: *A king is caught in tendrils [of hair]*.

Peshat: A Discourse Analysis

מלך אסור ברהטים

This final line of one of the lengthier *wasf* capitalizes on the former Solomonic vignettes. This woman conquers kings with a mere flick of her hair.

Song 8:11

In chapter 8 *Shlomo* is again a focal point for the poet. In this dramatic contrast the poet denigrates Solomon but idealizes the heroine.

כרם היה לשלמה בבעל המון

נתן את-הכרם לנטרים

איש יבא בפריו אלף כסף

כרמי שלי לפני

האלף לך שלמה ומאתים לנטרים את-פריו

> *Shlomo* had a vineyard in *Ba'al-Hamon* [lit. husband-of-a-multitude]
> He gave the vineyard to **watchmen**
> Each would receive for its fruit a thousand pieces of silver
> My vineyard is before me!
> To *Shlomo* is the thousand
> And the two hundred for the watchmen of its fruit . . .

Solomon is the owner of a vineyard. He has any number of laborers and watchmen to care for it.[104] The idea of money changing hands is fundamental to the vignette. This concept is repeated in the sequence. The heroine makes her claim. Her vineyard is her own, i.e., not to be worked by others, and not to be the subject of trade; a commodity. The vignette seems to take the form of a wisdom parable rather than a narrative of actual events.

Rather than *Shlomo*, the target of this wisdom may be the antagonistic brothers. They are the ones implied in the following verses of chapter 8 and who culturally have authority over their sister's marriage prospects and in cultures like this one, marriage offers do involve an economic exchange.

---

104. Note that watchmen [*notrim*] may be equated to keepers [*shomrim*] (Song 3:3, 5:7).

The heroine makes her claim for freedom culminating in the emphatic response in verse 12: *my vineyard is my own!* She is not the property of others.

Brothers

If villains do exist in the Song of Songs, they are the brothers[105] and male-others. Both male relatives and male-others are outsiders with respect to the protagonists. In the ancient Near East and in some contemporary societies, the male members of a family maintain an authority of law over the females of the household. This rule of law outlaws any non-legitimated relationships between the young women of the household and other men, except of course those vetted and approved by father or brothers. So also it seems in this text, that in lieu of the father who is absent in the Song, the sons rule over the sexuality of their sister.

Patriarchy does not provide much space for women who want to make decisions about their lives, or even those want to claim a right. Even a woman who wants justice, even that justice defined as just by social law, can be obstructed and dismissed. In the story of Judah and Tamar, Tamar is given to a sequence of sons as a wife and yet bears no heir for Judah's line. And while she is promised yet another husband by the patriarch Judah he seems to forget that she exists. Finally, in search of the right to have the security of a male descendant, she disguises herself and tricks Judah into sleeping with her. Of course 3 months later when the patriarch finds out that this daughter-in-law is pregnant without a living husband she is naturally, very speedily brought to judgement. Yet Judah's own fornication with a prostitute is of no significance in the narrative: *"Bring her out," said Judah, "and let her be burned."* (Gen 38:24).

Having a clandestine relationship without the approval of the male members of the family is risky indeed and it is exactly this sort of scenario that the *Shulamith* risks. In fact her brothers take preventative measures by keeping their sister "behind walls" and "behind doors" (Song 8:8) and deliberately impede their women's liberty to make choices.

---

105. The word brother only occurs once in the Song. This is in the sequence where the woman wishes her hero was her brother so she could kiss him (8:1). The brothers when referred to explicitly are called, (ironically), "sons of my mother" (1:6) and are indirectly implied in 8:8 when they refer to "our sister." This irony is discussed further later in this section.

In modern agrarian societies we see a correlating context (at least vastly more similar than the current western, urban existence).[106] In the film *Moolaade*, as a modern dramatic telling, we see an agrarian village in rural Senegal.[107] The film depicts a rural village scene, where men have almost complete control over the women of the village. Village decisions concerning women are made by the men, with only minimal input from the women concerned. These seem to prioritize patriarchal concerns before the needs or desires of the women. Any action from a woman that could destabilise this patriarchal control is immediately repressed by condemnation and punishment. The implication is that this maintenance of patriarchal rule keeps society in order. Women do evidence a voice but it is often behind the scenes, subversive, and in subterfuge rather than open, and is always, always risky.

The Hebrew Bible makes similar distinctions in Torah laws. Men are to keep control of their families.[108] Extended families were the core kinship groups of that society. With this background in mind, the Song is defiant in its protest.[109] The claim the *Shulamith* makes that *love is as strong as death* really does mean what it says because she does risk death by stoning if she is discovered in this lover's folly.[110]

It is instructive that there is no father-voice in the Song of Songs. Often what is not said in the Song can be as important as what is said. The poet of the Song of Songs uses silence with communicative intention. In Relevance Theory these silences are part of the manifest facts in the cognitive environment; absence of speech or action where speech or action is expected carries the weight of implied meaning. Fewell and Gunn note: "We recognize the force of silence in life, where failure or refusal to answer may be of utmost significance. No less is true of our text."[111] Silence carries its own weak implicatures that embed and enrich the text.

---

106. See also Shirazi, "The Sofreh."

107. Sembene, *Moolaade*.

108. Num 30, concerning women making vows; Deut 16, concerning women and worship; Deut 22:21ff., concerning women and their sexuality. Implicit in these laws are other controls: women are given in marriage and do not choose for themselves, their sexuality is owned, their voice also is owned by either father or husband.

109. The Song as a song of protest is explored in *Remez*.

110. Deut 22:21

111. Fewell and Gunn refer to Ruth rather than the Song of Songs but the concept is true of both books. Fewell and Gunn, *Compromising Redemption*, 17.

The brothers speak, by implication, in Song 8:8 and male-others in Song 6:13. Both these groups are referred to in third and fourth person at other times, but even more clearly with the contrasting prominence of Mother (and daughters) there is silence and absence of Father. This absence is implicit on the poet's part providing by absence, the profound disconnection of the daughter and father. He may disavow his daughter, or, she has chosen to disavow him. However, the concept of Father may be more relevant than searching for the identity of a particular individual. In the Song, Father by proxy represents authority, law, justice and judgment.[112] The *Shulamith*'s brothers appear to act on his behalf.

Song 1:6b

The Song is sometimes a cacophony of voice. The brothers are dramatic voices in the Song that interrupt the flow of the lovers' dialogue, breaking in and providing an important foil of tension. The poet may intend us to read the voices as actually spoken, but types of male speech role-played by the heroine or female companions are not uncommon even in modern song in agrarian societies, i.e., Sephardic Yemen, agrarian India and also rural Iranian women's song.[113]

The poet first begins to introduce the male other[s] in the Song in 1:6b. This verse is an address to the daughters of Jerusalem and features partially in the third section from that aspect. Here we look at it from the paradoxical perspective that the poet intends to make of the concept *brothers*. Here they are the children/sons of her mother, *banei'imi*, but they are angry, with no evident justification. The poet has these male relatives, as closely connected through the mother, but separated by their anger. In this first instance, they are clearly antagonists (paradoxically so). Underscoring this seems to be an indictment of the social ordering of the family. Kinship and connection should engender love and support, not anger.

---

112. Mother mentioned frequently in the Song represents love, romance, sexuality, birth, conception, nurturing and grace. These two representations meet in the vignette on Solomon's wisdom in 1 Kings 3:16–27. This vignette is explored in Trible, "Journey of a Metaphor," 31–33. The love of a mother in this case is one that transcends the requirement for justice. A mother simply wants her child to have life. She is less concerned with the need to be right.

113. Meyers, *Discovering Eve*, 31 and Sharaby, "The Bride's Henna Ritual," 22.

Peshat: A Discourse Analysis

אל-תראני שאני שחרחרת ששזפתני השמש
בני אמי נחרו-בי שמני נטרה את-הכרמים
כרמי שלי לא נטרתי

> Do not see me as black
> I have been pierced by the Sun's rays[114]
> The sons of my mother
> They scorched me [their anger blazed]
> They set me to watch over the vineyards
> My own vineyard I have not watched ...

Song 2:15

In this slip of prose the gender of the speaker is ambiguous, first person plural. *Shual* [jackals] are male in gender and may represent young men. Vineyards in the previous prose, have been distinctly related to the young woman, and by extension young women. In my analysis of the discourse, this prose bursts in on the love entreaties made by the hero. The heroine who continues their dialogue after this interruption seems unperturbed by it.

The fact that it is a disruption seems best allocated to the dramatic, antagonistic voices of the brothers, who may want to scare away these jackals or even catch and kill them. If it refers to the hero then it denigrates and diminishes him in contrast to the heroine's overt adoration. It signals the non-legitimacy of their love. It is un-supported by the heroine's male relatives. The way in which the outsider speech bursts into and interrupts the love discourse signals a backdrop in which there is the possibility of violence. It serves the Song by intensifying the drama and background tension. It heightens the fragility of the heroine's love.

אחזו-לנו שעלים קטנים
מחבלים כרמים וכרמינו סמדר

> Seize for us the little *jackals*
> *Vine-spoilers!*
> When our vines blossom ...

---

114. Lit. Don't look at me, for I am dark, burned by the sun.

Earthing the Cosmic Queen

Song 6:13

It's hard to imagine brothers watching their sister dance. In this case, the male outsider voices seem most likely to be male-others in the village or city.[115] There is a disconnection between these others and the *Shulamith* in the way they call out to her. This calling out seems an objectification of the *Shulamith's* body that is discomforting in comparison to the luxuriousness and tenderness of the *wasf*. Do the village men only see an object of lust, or entertainment: *shuvi, shuvi!* This poverty of connection between these particular players and the *Shulamith* features to heighten the rich connectedness of the two lovers who love the external but also the internal: the voice, the friendship and thoughts they share.

שובי שובי השולמית

שובי שובי ונחזה-בך

מה-תחזו בשולמית כמחלת המחנים

> Turn, turn Shulamith
> Turn, turn
> So we can fix our eyes on you
> Why should you gaze at Shulamith
> Like a dancer in a festival?

The daughters of Jerusalem, if they are indeed the voices speaking in retort here, share our indignation that the heroine should be treated so, and they reply with this accusation to the male-outsiders who stare but fail to perceive.[116]

Song 8:1

This is not an interruption by a brother's voice but the entreaty of the heroine and with it the poet explores another facet of the heroine's willingness

---

115. These "male others" are mentioned more than once in the Song. The brothers "little jackals" slogan (ch. 1) may be directed at them. Again in 8:8 the brothers disdain suitors (male-others).

116. Note the different emphasis here than to the women's invitation to look and perceive *Shlomo's* mother and his wedding crown in chapter 3. Recall Isaiah 6 on listening but not hearing, seeing but not perceiving.

to sacrifice just to be near the one she loves. This is the first time the poet refers to the male relative as *ach*.

מי יתנך כאח לי

יונק שדי אמי

אמצאך בחוץ אשקך גם לא-יבזו לי:

In this excerpt the poet twists the disconnected relationship between the heroine and her male relatives to one with the potential to become liberating. Some brother-sister relationships may not only be about violence, anger and control, but also affection:

> What I would give
> If you were my brother
> That you once sucked the breast of my mother
> I would find you in the street
> I would kiss you
> And no one would bring me to shame . . .

In the following lines this brother-sister affection crosses boundaries into the taboo.[117] At many points, the poet's heroine becomes almost an iconoclast of certain prohibitions instituted in the Torah in her belief that her love transcends.[118]

אנהגך אביאך אל-בית אמי

תלמדני אשקך מיין הרקח מעסים רמגי

שמאלו תחת ראשי וימנו תחבקני

> I would lead you
> I would bring you to my mother's house, she will teach me
> I will pour for you, spiced wine
> My pomegranate's sweet juice
> —His left hand under my head
> And his right hand embraces me

---

117. This is not uncommon in comparative literature. See Scott, "Radha in the Erotic Play of the Universe," 239–42, and also Landy, "The Song of Songs and the Garden of Eden," 522, 527–28.

118. For example the prohibitions in Lev 18:9 "The nakedness of your sister—your father's daughter or your mother's, whether born into the household or outside—do not uncover their nakedness."

With the closing refrain the eroticism of the verse is incendiary.

Song 8:8

The flow of chapter 8 breaks at verse eight where the poet appears to stage an interruption of speech again from the sons of the mother. This little piece of prose has a strong connection to the first chapter of the Song (1:6) and forms an inclusio around the entire song.

אחות לנו קטנה ושדים אין לה

מה-נעשה לאחתנו ביום שידבר-בה

אם-חומה היא נבנה עליה טירת כסף

ואם-דלת היא נצור עליה לוח ארז

> We have a little sister and she has no breasts
> What will we do with her
> When she is spoken with [by suitors]?[119]
> This wall will be fortified with silver
> This door we will barricade with a cedar beam . . .

The heroine interjects boldly:

אני חומה ושדי כמגדלות

אז הייתי בעיניו כמוצאת שלום

> I am a wall
> And my breasts are towers
> Then I was in his eyes as one who finds *shalom* . . .

Once again, we find the voice of the brothers and a defiant response by the heroine. She affirms her love for this man, a love that her brothers appear to denigrate, as if it mattered not to them that she is in love, but only that she obeys them. The allusion to some kind of imprisonment is frightening. It is as if, in the event she follows her desire, she will be the subject of judgment proportional to how greatly they may feel their honor is impugned.

There is an example in the books of the prophet Samuel (2 Sam 20:3) in which ten concubines who were raped and degraded by the powerful

---

119. 1 Sam 25:39 has a similar use of *dabar b'* . . . David *spoke with* Abigail.

Peshat: A Discourse Analysis

usurper, Absalom, were literally boarded and sealed up in a room by David when he returned to power. Thus even events beyond women's power to control may mean a truly horrible judgment. With this in mind, the *Shulamith* is truly brave or truly reckless. She rejects the authority of her male relatives. She refuses to be their possession. She appears to risk it all because *I am his and he is mine* (Song 2:16, 6:3, 7:10).

The aggressive male relatives, male-others and the presence of the silent Father (foregrounded by his absence) perform a significant function in the Song. They provide the poet with the necessary apparatus of antagonism that in the Song of Songs frames the even more wonderful liberation of love for which the heroine strives.

Losing and Finding

The most poignant of thematic developments in the Song are the vignettes that feature sequences of *losing and finding*. The strongest representatives of this locale in the Song occur in two primary sections, in chapters 3 and 5, but the imagery of *losing and finding* is threaded into the other locales we have identified in the Song and continues to appear explicitly and ubiquitously.[120]

The poet employs the phrase *sh'ahavah nafshi* as a schema that routinely links these explicit events invoking the concept of losing or finding. I interpret this phrase as *the one I love with all my breath*. In this I try to avoid the dualistic division of the human being into physical body and spiritual soul. In Hebrew, *nefesh* is the spark of life, which is inseparable from the carnal act of breathing.[121]

---

120. For example, even at the stage of entreaty (level 1) we sense the heroine's profound desire for what she does not yet have. Her entreaty is an expression of her desire to seek out and possess this entity.

121. Such as that when YHWH breathed the breath of life into the human in Genesis 2:7 and the human became a "breathing creature."

The first introduction of loss, and the work of finding, arises in the very first lines. And a slip of prose in the final chapter seems to perfectly conclude this crucial thread.

Song 1:7–8

The poet introduces this idea of losing and finding in chapter 1 with the heroine who has made her first claim against the male relatives and now, with her position firm, she asks "Where is he?" as if to follow her claim with action. She has made up her mind to join him. His response seems abstract, perhaps cruel or perhaps a lover's teasing. Regardless, the frustration of separation is palpable. The poet hides the hero's location from the heroine, and his speech is purposefully ambiguous. There is no sure hope of consummation here, just the unbearable tension of trying to find that lost thing, and angst over whether perhaps the beloved does not want to be found.

הגידה לי שאהבה נפשי

איכה תרעה

איכה תרביץ בצהרים

שלמה אהיה כעטיה על עדרי חבריך

> Tell me
> I love you with all my breath
> Where are you grazing
> Where are you resting during the hot sun of noon
> I would be shamed if I came upon your friend's flocks

In the hope of providing relevance here, where the wording in Hebrew is obscure, I have used a dynamic equivalent in translation. The phrase *c'otyah* is literally "like one veiled"; possibly a prostitute. This is how she would appear if she followed her lover's taunt, wandered out alone searching for him; coming up to each of the shepherds and asking if her lover was there. *I would be shamed if I came upon your friend's flocks* expresses what seems to be the intent.

The hero's words here are unexpected. Instead of clear directions or a welcoming acceptance of her: "Here I am, come!" He tells her to do the very thing she must not do.

Peshat: A Discourse Analysis

אִם-לֹא תֵדְעִי לָךְ הַיָּפָה בַּנָּשִׁים צְאִי-לָךְ בְּעִקְבֵי הַצֹּאן
וּרְעִי אֶת-גְּדִיֹּתַיִךְ עַל מִשְׁכְּנוֹת הָרֹעִים

If you don't know
Most beautiful one
Follow in the sheep-trails
Pasture your kids by the shepherd's tents . . .

Is he there? Is he teasing her? Is he putting her to shame, putting her to a test? Why is he not there to meet her? Why must she be the one to have faith? But perhaps in the context the shepherds, his friends, are also her friends. Perhaps they are insiders/comrades and she is safe there. But, this seems unrealistic given the social setting and that the poet must be readily aware of the expectations or presumptions of a Hebrew audience in matters of male/female honor and shame. Does her hero suggest that if she brings young goats with her she is not appearing like a veiled woman making rounds of the shepherd's tents.[122]

This repartee is unsettling and the chance of danger, risk and humiliation seems close.

Song 3:1–4

The vignette of chapter 3 is the first of the two major losing/finding sequences. In this dramatic narrative, the poet sets the *Shulamith* in her home, at night on her bed. The heroine lies there in great angst as her desire for her hero becomes untenable. Is it real or a dream when she courts danger by wandering through the darkened city alone in search of him? The poet employs the word *baqash* persistently in this sequence. All at once the word means to desire, to yearn for and to seek, and it seems to be used fittingly across the spectrum of its semantic range. The word embodies the mental yearning and the physical act of going.

עַל-מִשְׁכָּבִי בַּלֵּילוֹת בִּקַּשְׁתִּי אֵת שֶׁאָהֲבָה נַפְשִׁי
בִּקַּשְׁתִּיו וְלֹא מְצָאתִיו

122. In Ruth, we see the implied danger of a woman alone in the field, i.e., Ruth 2:9, See also Deut 22:25 and since a field is a good deal nearer the safety of the village/city than the grasslands of the shepherds it could be imagined the danger to the lone woman is even greater.

Earthing the Cosmic Queen

> On my bed, by night
> I yearned for him
> The one I love with all my breath
> I sought him but did not find him . . .

> אקומה נא ואסובבה בעיר
>
> בשוקים וברחבות
>
> אבקשה את שאהבה נפשי
>
> בקשתיו ולא מצאתיו

> I must rise now and circle the city
> [Ascend] the streets and [go up to] the plaza
> I will search for the one I love with all my breath
> I sought him but could not find him.

> מצאוני השמרים הסבבים בעיר
>
> את שאהבה נפשי ראיתם

> The guardians found me
> The ones that surround the city
> Have any of you seen the one I love with all my breath?

> כמעט שעברתי מהם עד שמצאתי את שאהבה נפשי
>
> אחזתיו ולא ארפנו עד-שהביאתיו
>
> אל-בית אמי ואל-חדר הורתי

> It was a little after that
> When I found the one I love with all my breath
> I held him and would not let go
> Until we came to my mother's house
> The chamber of the one who awoke me to life . . .[123]

The repetition of *sh'ahavah nafshi* intensifies the vignette. The identification of her hero, as embedded in the core of her being gives further rise to the mood of desperation. Social norms are deprioritised and she loses all inhibition. The heroine's words pour out unchecked until they reach the plateau of verse four. At this summit point, the sense of relief is palpable, though she still holds tight. The lovers reach the sanctuary of the Mother's

---

123. Lit. "of she who in bearing bore me."

room, perhaps the poet hints at her womb here, which would link the scene to the life-giving, nurturing quality of maternity.

Song 5:2–7, 8b

Chapter 5 contains the second of the two critical losing/finding sequences. This is a similar dramatic narration of the story of the search, however the story has new twists and turns and an alternate outcome. The recurrent characters in the narrative are the hero who comes close this time, audible but still not visible; and the heroine in the act of searching, still in torment, with the city streets and the guardians still in play.

The heroine is in her bedroom. It is a darkened scene. She is in a state of unrest. She sleeps but her core (her heart) is conscious; awake, unsleeping. She hears his voice, audibly, or perhaps as a figment of her dreams. If it is a dream—and the twists, turns, the fading in and out of imagery and characters seem to indicate it is—then this dream is a nightmare.

אני ישנה ולבי ער

קול דודי דופק

I sleep but my heart is awake
The voice of my lover knocks . . .

פתחי-לי אחתי רעיתי יונתי תמתי

שראשי נמלא-טל קוצותי רסיסי לילה

[Masc] Open to me, my sister, my friend
My dove, my perfect[124] one
For my head is saturated with dew
and my hair with the damp night mist . . .

פשטתי את-כתנתי איככה אלבשנה

רחצתי את-רגלי איככה אטנפם

[Fem] I laid out my robe
Should I dress again?
I have bathed my feet
Should I soil them?

---

124. Lit. "flawless."

Earthing the Cosmic Queen

דודי שלח ידו מן-החור ומעי המו עליו

My lover stretched out his hand, through the opening
And deep inside I seethed for him . . .

קמתי אני לפתח לדודי וידי נטפו-מור
ואצבעתי מור עבר על כפות המנעול

I arose to open to my lover
And my hands oozed myrrh
And my fingers pure myrrh on the clasps

פתחתי אני לדודי

ודודי חמק עבר

נפשי יצאה בדברו

בקשתיהו ולא מצאתיהו

קראתיו ולא ענני

I opened to my lover
But my lover had vanished [into the mist]
When he spoke I couldn't breathe
I searched for him but couldn't find him
I cried out to him, but he didn't answer me . . .

מצאני השמרים הסבבים בעיר

הכוני פצעוני

נשאו את-רדידי מעלי

שמרי החמות

The guardians found me, those that surround the city
They struck me, bruised me
They tore off my veil [*redidi*]
Those guardians of the walls . . .

השבעתי אתכם בנות ירושלם
אם-תמצאו את-דודי מה-תגידו לו שחולת אהבה אני

Swear to me [completely!]!
All of you daughters of Jerusalem

> If you find my lover
> Tell him I am grief-stricken over love ...

In this vignette, the poet seems to have the heroine enact an alternate response to her burgeoning desire. The heroine is hesitant initially, appearing to question the value of risking anything for her lover, positing justifications for not encountering him: having to dress, having to walk. Considering the lengths to which she has previously extended herself in the first sequence of this kind, the new dilemma is frustrating for the reader. Open the door!!!! In the former sequence, the hero was the passive one, in limbo, and she was able to take hold of him.[125]

The *Shulamith*'s hero is *nearly* proactive in this sequence, somehow able to stretch his arm right through her door into her boudoir (dangerously close) but still not able to touch her. It's terribly exciting and she can't stop herself moving towards him. But it's too late, she can't get the door open and he withdraws. It's a devastating misstep, and the hero fades away, becoming lost in the same mist that dampened his hair. The *Shulamith*, now active in the sequence, is full of regret, profoundly feeling her loss, in order to preserve clean feet. That kind of purity seems trivial now and "unclean" in contrast to this great, messy, wonderful, actualizing love. The poet's ability to manipulate mood in this sequence is ornate and skilful.

The poet does not stop here. The abuse by the *shomrim* [keepers, guardians, watchmen], following the sequence regarding cleanliness, *tehor* (clean) and the now-missing hero, the flight through Jerusalem's streets, might point to the priests who are often labelled the *Shomrei haBayit* [the guardians of the house]?[126] The prophets also take the title *Shomrim* in the Hebrew bible.[127] If this is the destination of the poet's implicature, why is she painting such a brutal portrait? These watchmen cannot see at all.[128]

It is fitting that at the end of this complex and nuanced film noir scene, the poet has the heroine recrudesce the ritual vow to the young women. This time however *Shulamith* is grief-stricken. She missed her chance. The

---

125. Ironically, in the prior sequence, the heroine, when she had located her lover "took hold and brought him," was able to possess him. In this sequence the hero is stretching out towards the *Shulamith* but is unable to achieve his desire to "take hold and bring her." The actual act of possessing (aligned with men in the Hebrew Bible, see Deut 22:29; 21:11; Exod 20:17; 21:10) in this instance is in the power of the woman. She imaginatively repeats this feat in 8:1–2.

126. See Eccl 12:3; Jer 52:24; Ezek 40:46; 44:8, 14.

127. Isa 62:6 as one example.

128. See the *Remez* chapter on the topic of Sleeping and Waking.

lovers are star-cross'd. It is the "almost" of the encounter that is hardest to bear.

Song 6:1

This question that is put in the mouth of the daughters of Jerusalem is also considered in a prior section (the locale of the daughters). Here the voices of the daughters are drawn to the heroine's quest. These are the same young women who alternately echo and also perhaps restrain the voice of the heroine. They too have subsequently reconsidered the worth of the heroine's love.

אנה הלך דודך היפה בנשים

אנה פנה דודך ונבקשנו עמך

> Where has your lover gone
> Most beautiful of women?
> Which way did he turn
> And we will search with you?

Song 8:1

This site of *losing and finding* rises within other themes. This time the paradigms of *losing and finding* and *the brothers* intersect. At this point in the Song the theme of *mother* also coalesces. In a twist the poet aligns all three. The brothers are part of the quest but only because by their refusal they have catalyzed her action. The heroine associates her hero-lover here by an odd triangulation of tropes: brothers, mother, lover. The heroine, desperate for realization of her dream, imagines a fantasy scenario, where the lover is her brother. Again the mother is present here, providing sustenance, wisdom and life. But this plan is no plan. Her lover is not her brother. Even if he was, to pursue a sexual relationship would be taboo. Of course it's figurative. She merely wishes him close by any means. They would be forever together but forever separate or forever condemned.[129]

---

129. I mean that within the laws of Torah incest is strictly forbidden (Lev 18:9). If he becomes her "real" brother they could be always together but never as "one flesh." The punishment for such an "abomination" is exile (Lev 18:29).

Peshat: A Discourse Analysis

מי יתנך כאח לי יונק שדי אמי

אמצאך בחוץ אשקך גם לא-יבזו לי

אנהגך אביאך אל-בית אמי

תלמדני אשקך מיין הרקח מעסיס רמני

> What I would give
> If you were like my brother
> That you nursed at my mother's breast
> I would find you in the streets
> If I kissed you no one would bring me to shame
> I would lead you
> And bring you to my mother's house
> She would teach me
> I will pour out for you, spiced wine
> My pomegranate's sweet juice . . .

Song 8:10

In the heroine's response, again to the antagonists (the brothers), the poet inserts a *dal segno* to the theme of losing and finding. In this instance the conscious act of naming herself, and setting herself in opposition to the names society might give her, has the direct effect in her world. The poet crafts a sense of immediacy into this soliloquy through a sudden temporal-spatial shift that seems to have awakened both *Shulamith* and her hero: *az hayiti' v'ainiv c'mozet shalom*. She recounts, and in doing so has woken an epiphany.

אני חומה ושדי כמגדלות

אז הייתי בעיניו כמוצאת שלום

> I am a wall
> And my breasts are towers
> Then I was in his eyes
> As one who finds *shalom* . . .

97

The theme of *losing and finding* is strongly represented and repeated by the poet in the context of the heroine's growing sense of and response to her love. In a myriad of ways the poet has woven the concept of *journey*, the journeying that is intrinsic to love, throughout the entire song. In the final lines of the Song, the heroine seems to have found the *Garden*, the destination, and made it her home. In contrast, her hero is still journeying, but he is at the very least listening for her voice.

In the Garden

In this particular analysis, the *Garden* thematic or locale is the western horizon of the poem topographically. It is the goal or destination of the poet's message, the place of the setting sun. The poet does not to go beyond it. The garden is the place where *shalom* is found. The garden seems to signify the true home of the *Shulamith* as in chapter 8:13 at the conclusion of the Song places her there, albeit alone. This garden is the place where love is made (literally or figuratively), but more than this, it is the place where the beauty, intimacy, wholesomeness, totality or vitality of human relationship is experienced or imagined. The desire of the heroine to experience this wholeness of human relationship is also a singular aim. She does not settle for what society might deem sufficient for a young woman that is to make the most of what is offered to her, accept her lot. Her sights are set at the very summit of human passion. She expects the earth, and this is celebrated by the poet. The poet undoubtedly validates and empowers this idea of searching for more; more from life itself.

The Song is dynamic and the text ebbs and flows between its core imagery and locales. There are many such surges outwards to the *Garden* throughout the Song, using implicatures or direct reference. There are also constant hints and echoes within the other locales. There are ten vignettes in the Song where the Garden is in vibrant focus for the poet. *Garden* embodies the concept of home at the end of the long journey. This destination is the place of wholeness, the place of the fullness and the emptying of desire.[130] The first garden scene is in chapter 1.

---

130. Walsh, *Exquisite Desire*, 3. Walsh's journey into the world of the Song of Songs is fascinating and compelling. She sees "desire" or even "lust" (in the manner of the lust for life) as the key to unlocking the Song's meaning.

Peshat: A Discourse Analysis

Song 1:13–14

The poet places the heroine in the heady embrace of her royal lover. The two lie together on a couch in a luxuriously appointed chamber. The poet makes us feel vicariously, through the words of the heroine, the onshore evening breeze from the Mediterranean flowing through the ornate latticework. Through the heroine's description we sense the warmth of the day gently exuding from the stonework, from unclothed, entangled human bodies. We understand the heat in the room causes the sprinkled fragrant oils to diffuse throughout the room. The fragrance of myrrh is dense in the air making the room, the couch and the embrace even more close, intimate and intense. The heroine loses herself and finds herself in the embrace and the experience brings a new epiphany of her beloved other. This is a *Garden* epiphany. She finds *shalom*, richness in living that she has never experienced before.

צרור המר דודי לי בין שדי ילין

אשכל הכפר דודי לי בכרמי עין גדי

    A parcel of myrrh is my lover to me
    Between my breasts he rests [through the night]
    A spray of henna is my lover to me
    In the vineyards of Ein Gedi . . .

Song 2:1–3

In this vignette the poet makes the reader privy to interaction between the two protagonists. With a coquette tone, the poet has the heroine compare herself to common flowers such as the *chavzel* and the *shoshan*. The hero dramatically contrasts the heroine with other women: *c'shoshenet bain ha'cochim*. In return the heroine echoes the sentiment with a panegyric using different imagery (though still agricultural/natural imagery). He is figuratively a prince among men, a *tapuach b'eytzei ha'hyazei ha'yaar*. He bears fruit while all other trees are useful only for building and burning.

אני חבצלת השרון שושנת העמקים

כשושנת בין החוחים כן רעיתי בין הבנות

כתפוח בעצי היערי היער כן דודי בין הבנים

בצלו חמדתי וישבתי ופריו מתוק לחכי

Earthing the Cosmic Queen

[Fem.] I am a crocus of the Sharon, a lotus of the valleys [Masc.]
—Like a lotus among thistles so is my darling friend among the daughters
—Like a [fruiting] apricot among the woodland trees
This is my lover among the sons
In his shadow i desire to make my home
His fruit is sweet in my mouth

The poet develops a short narrative where the young lovers are suddenly transported to a house of wine. The hero is proactive in this scene. He brings her there. His love is declared. Yet the narrator of the scene is the heroine.

הביאני אל-בית היין ודגלו עלי אהבה

... He has brought me to the house of wine
And his standard over me is love ...

The heroine as narrator reveals this vignette as *dream* in the following verse. The poet has her fall back to entreaty as she voices what is hope rather than reality.

סמכוני באשישות

רפדוני בתפוחים

כי-חולת אהבה אני

Lie me down with caked-raisons
Let me recline with apricots
For afflicted with love am I

What is now clearly soliloquy and not discourse between characters trails away with the heroine's tragic wish that she was in his very intimate embrace. There is sadness that she can only dream of this tryst:

שמאלו תחת לראשי וימינו תחבקני

His left hand under my head
His right hand embraces me ...

These lines thus cast some doubt on the reality of any of the encounters between the lovers. Is the poet indicating it is all a dream?[131]

131. The following verse (2:7) confirms that this is a monologue/soliloquy by the heroine in the presence of the daughters and not actually taking place with her hero. The mood is one of anguish making the account a reverie or more likely an imaginative

Peshat: A Discourse Analysis

Song 4:12–16; 5:1

In chapter 4 the poet returns strongly to garden scenes after a lengthy *wasf* on the beauty and strength of the heroine. In these vignettes, the poet, in the purest sense yet, presents the heroine as the metaphorical garden. The poet introduces another representation for the heroine almost immediately which has the effect of intensifying the garden imagery. She is *gal na'ul / ma'ayn chatum*. At first the poet has the hero narrate about his heroine in third person. The reader and hero are distanced and excluded by both the person (i.e., third person) and the repetition of words like *closed* and *sealed* (*na'ul* repeated twice and a synonym *chatum*). The consequent contrast is heightened by the clever change in part of speech. The narration shifts in viewpoint addressing the heroine as "you" and introducing the possibility of overcoming obstacles by words such as *shalach*. The heroine stretches out or branches out, freeing herself from restraints. This is symbolized by the irrepressible flux of her fragrant aromatics and perfumes that cannot be closed up or sealed up or bottled. These spices and resins, when caught by the wind, spill over their bounds.

גן נעול אחתי כלה

גל נעול מעין חתום

שלחיך פרדס רימונים עם פרי מגדים

כפרים עם-נרדים

נרד וכרכם קנה וקנמון עם כל-עצי לבנון

מור ואהלות עם כל-ראשי בשמים

> A garden enclosed is my sister, my bride
> a spring enclosed
> a fountain sealed
> [but] you branch out [like a] grove of pomegranates with
> a treasure of fruit
> Henna with nard
> Nard and saffron
> Calamus and cinnamon
> all the frankincense trees
> Myrrh and aloes and all the finest balsam

---

anticipation or a dream. Again, as a comparison, in the Yemen Sephardic culture brides and their companions sing songs about the return of an "unknown lover." Sharaby, "The Bride's Henna Ritual," 22.

The poet capitalizes on the liberating and overflowing of these positive, fragrant elements. Now the heroine plays the narrator as she affirms grandly her desire to be free to love.

מעין גנים באר מים חיים ונזלים מן-לבנון

> A fountain of gardens
> a spring of living waters
> and flowing streams from the white mountain . . .

The poet presents the heroine as an open fountain, a producing, open spring, a flowing stream. She rejects all societal and personal constraints. She is living water.

At the climax of this sequence on the woman-garden, the poet has the heroine call out to the north and south winds to give her release and upon which her inhibited passions, figured as perfumes, signal with their scent her readiness to reunite with her lover, and her desire to be completely consumed by him.

עורי צפון ובואי תימן הפיחי גני יזלו בשמיו

יבא דודי לגנו ויאכל פרי מגדיו

> Awake Zaphon, and Come Taeman!
> Breathe into my garden, let my perfumes stream
> let my lover come to his garden
> and consume its treasure of fruit

For the final vignette in this sequence of garden scenes, the poet allows the hero to reply once more, speaking in first person. The reader perceives love through the hero's eyes. This vignette is slightly disconnected from the other three. The hero speaks in past tense. His actions are complete. Or does the poet have the heroine reflecting on the words her hero might say after the consummation of their love? The hero does not name the heroine. There are no endearments as in the former vignette. The poet develops the intent of the lines via metaphor and connotation, each stich subsequent to the initial line occurs in a pair: myrrh with balsam, wild honey with pure, wine with milk. There is a play on numbers figuratively in the Song. Halves becoming whole, references to all the twos recoursing to one. This might be a veiled reference to the parity of their consummation, the two-ness of their meeting and that every delight has been sampled.

Peshat: A Discourse Analysis

The vignette concludes with an appeal outwards to outsiders. The hero appeals to all lovers, all new friends and old, and you, reader, having invested in the couple are included. There is a subtext here that seems to urge the reader not to be satisfied with a commonplace existence but to suck the very marrow of life.

באתי לגני אחתי כלה
אריתי מורי עם-בשמי
אכלתי יערי עם-דבשי
שתיתי ייני עם-חלבי
אכלו רעים שתו
ושכרו דודים

> I have descended into my garden
> I have harvested my myrrh with my balsam
> I have eaten my wild honey with my pure honey
> I have drunk my wine with my milk
> —Feast, comrades! Drink!
> Drink deeply lovers!

Song 6:2

The poet returns to the garden theme in chapter 6. This vignette is an echo of the previous garden scene. This time the hero's words are echoed by the heroine still from his perspective as the proactive player who comes and eats. The hero passes through those same balsam trees but this destination is his life work (no longer his sheep in the field). He shepherds in these gardens and harvests lotus. The heroine is willing but passive in both vignettes.

דודי ירד לגנו לערגות הבשם
לרעות בגנים וללקט שושנים

> My lover descended into his garden
> [Through] terraces of balsam
> To shepherd in the gardens, and harvest the lotus ...

Earthing the Cosmic Queen

Song 6:11–12

Once again the poet has the hero *descend* into the garden. That he goes down into has the connotation of love making. This scene this time ensues with a purpose. The lover comes down with motive. He wants to see how much this garden has awakened.

אל-גנת אגוז ירדתי
לראות באבי הנחל
לראות הפרחה הגפן
הנצו נרמנים

> [Masc.] Into the grove of walnuts I descended
> To see the lushness of the streams
> To see the budding vines
> The blossoming pomegranates

It is not clear which voice the poet intends for the next part. With such a precedence of interplay of discourse between the two protagonists prior to this point it fits that the heroine might now interject. In reply to the hero's purposed garden visit above, the heroine answers, *lo yadati nafshi*. She did not know herself. She did not know that her passion had risen to such heights. Nor did she know that she could love this man and have that love requited.

לא ידעתי נפשי שמתני מרכבות עמי נדיב

> [Fem.] I did not know my own passion
> It set me in the chariots of my people's prince

Song 7:8–14

The garden-oasis scene of chapter 7 is openly panegyric. Once again the hero is proactive. The poet has him explore the heroine with his eyes, writing a semi-*wasf*. He associates her body with a palm and her breasts with dates. He speaks to her directly using second person but it may be siloquy. As he speaks, he shifts to third person to speak of the heroine. She is the object of his desire. The visual stimulation arouses his ardour further as he envisions via metaphor, pressing against her body, holding her tightly, as if to climb into her.

מה-יפית ומה-נאמת אהבה בתאמוגים

זאת קומתך דמתה לתמר ושדיך לאשכלות

אמרתי אעלה בתמר אחזה בסנסניו

[How beautiful and how enchanting, love
Daughter of ecstasy]
This stature of yours is the resemblance of a palm
And your breasts as its fruit-clusters
I said to myself I shall ascend the palm
I shall take hold in its crown of fronds ...

At the next step in the sequence the hero returns to second person. The heroine is not collapsed into a collection of parts but becomes the beloved other again, but in continuation of the theme the focus remains on her breasts, though this is more explicitly defined. The visual focus (touching with the eye) becomes sensual (touching the body with hands), the background imagery of date clusters signals the touching/eating with the mouth as the scene clarifies. The scene is unbearably intimate when he tastes the inside of her mouth.

ויהיו-נא שדיך כאשכלות הגפן

וריח אפך כתפוחים

וחכך כיין הטוב

Let your breasts be like the grape-clusters on the vines
And your breath's fragrance like apricots
And inside your mouth like good wine ...

The poet interrupts the hero's discourse as the heroine meeting the hero's reverie measure for measure, utters a truly enigmatic line. *Shulamith*'s response here could evoke more than one interpretation. If it is sexual innuendo, it is startling, or, has the reader been primed to now read into each metaphor too far. The heroine's speech does conceivably signal a more active role here. Does the poet infer that she now takes the lead in their lovemaking?[132]

132. Potentially the author moves from the focus on the lips of the mouth (implied

Earthing the Cosmic Queen

הולך לדודי למישרים דובב שפתי ישנים

> [fem.] It flows to my lover smoothly
> It stirs lips that sleep ...

The sequence concludes with a variation on a refrain. The poet has the heroine recognize and validate the hero's desire for her. This seems to be an empowering recognition. In Genesis 3:16 a similar verse appears however this is not set in a positive light. The poet seems to redeem the words of Genesis 3:16 pointedly and the heroine is now in a position of power.

אני לדודי ועלי תשוקתו

> I am my lover's
> And upon me is his desire ...

At this point the poet changes the scenario. There is a slight disconnection as rather than further the imagery of consummation the reader is brought back again to its prelude. The poet now has the heroine entreaty the hero to set out on their journey to finally consummating their love.

לכה דודי נצא השדה נלינה בכפרים

נשכימה לכרמים

נראה אם-פרחה הגפן

פתח הסמדר

הנצו ברמונים

שם אתן את-דדי לך

הדודאים נתנו-ריח

> Come my lover
> Let us go away to the field
> We will pass the night in the henna
> At daybreak we will make for the vineyards
> We will see if the vines are budding, showing blossoms
> Red bursts of pomegranate flower
> There I will give my love to you
> The scent of mandrakes fills the air ...

---

in her breath's fragrance), both taste and aroma, to perhaps the lips of the vulva. The metaphor-rich language evokes a scandalously intimate image of deep arousal.

Peshat: A Discourse Analysis

The poet has her heroine peak in her attempts to persuade the hero to come. With the mention of mandrakes there is promise of magical love.

ועל-פתחינו כל-מגדים חדשים גם-ישנים

דודי צפנתי לך

> ... and at our gates
> Treasures [of fruit] of every kind
> New and old
> My lover I have stored up, for you[133]

Song 8:2–3

In between the prior garden scenes, the poet has the heroine wish for a meeting with her hero and even that he was kin so she could meet him openly. This is a strong implication that their love is not socially accepted. She is unable to meet him openly. The constraints of society cannot be avoided, and perhaps the only aide is that of her mother.[134] The heroine explores this possibility here as part of her urgency that they should be together and consummate their love. This also echoes a similar sequence in chapter 3 when the heroine brings her lost lover into her mother's house.

אנהגך אביאך אל-בית אמי

תלמדני אשקך מיין הרקח מעסיס רמני

> I would lead you
> And bring you into my mother's house
> My teacher
> I would satiate you with mulled wine
> The fresh, sweet wine of my pomegranate ...

The heroine's refrain seems to resonate with desperate hope.

שמאלו תחת ראשי וימינו תחבקני

> ... his left hand under my head
> And his right embraces me ...

---

133. See Matt 13:52
134. The significance of mothers is explored in the section: Mothers and the Garden.

Earthing the Cosmic Queen

Song 8:5b

The poet changes tack. The heroine is attributed with an alternate source of power to that of the warrior in Song 3:7–8. The poet invokes the power of mothers. In chapter 3 it was the heroine's mother who birthed her and awoke her to life. In this account it is the hero's mother who births the hero into life. In this the heroine is also a party. She is the one who awoke him with the same power as the one who birthed him. She represents generations of women who are mothers of life and have an innate power that transcends that of patriarchy. This power is centred in the garden.

. . . תחת בתפוח עוררתיך

שמה חבלתך אמך שמה חבלה ילדתך

> Beneath the apricot tree I awoke you
> There your mother travailed for you
> There she wrested and [awoke you to life].

Song 8:13a

At the end of the Song, the poet leaves her readers far from satisfaction. The hero recognises *Shulamith* is in the garden and he asks her to call out. We can see her but perhaps she can only hear us. She is cut off from all of us by this language that places her in there. We are on the outside. In this light all other scenes of consummation seem to be anticipatory, even imaginary. The reader is left in the primary state of desire with all its angst, not in psychological rest.

היושבת בגנים

חברים מקשיבים לקולך השמיעני . . .

> Woman, living in the gardens
> Comrades listen for your voice—let me hear it . . .

Mothers and the Garden

While Father is conspicuous by his absence in the Song, the poet makes Mother all the more conspicuous by her pervasive presence.

Peshat: A Discourse Analysis

The Song carries seven repeated references to *'im* [mother] in the Song. In two instances the mother is the *mother of sons* and in two instances references to mother are doubled in the same line signalling intensification. On one occasion (Song 3:4) references to mother are tripled. All this is evidence suggesting that the concept of mother plays an important role that shapes meaning in the Song. The mother shares a special relationship with the heroine, her home or room (perhaps womb) being implied here. Focus on the mother's ability to birth is the substance of two references. Both the hero and heroine owe their awakening to life to their birthing mothers. The first half of the final chapter of the Song sees a proliferation in references to "mother" (both the hero's and the heroine's) with five hemistichs devoted to their description (8:1b, 2a, 2b, 5b, 5c). With these repeated references the poet shows clearly her desire to draw attention to the significance of the concept for the Song.

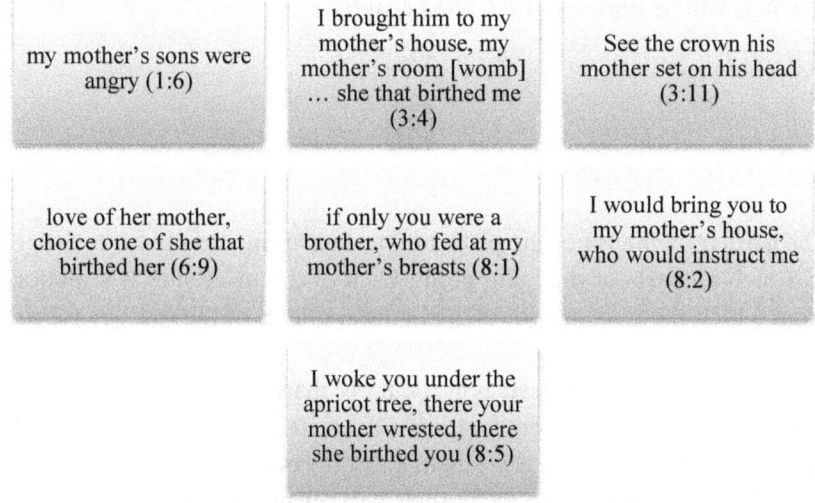

Figure 4: References to "mother" in the Song of Songs

The brothers, who are antagonists in the Song clearly at two points (1:6 in third/fourth person and 8:8–9 in first) are also the sons of the mother, who in other parts of the same song represents liberation, wisdom and life. From a pragmatic point of view, there may be irony intended here. The paradox of womanhood is that *a woman births the men who rule her*. With the pervasive use of the "mother" motif the poet may be suggesting that women are empowered through their sexuality, passion and life-giving potential. Does this suggest tacit acceptance of this power on the part of the audience receiving the Song or does the Song hope to win the audience to a concept of female empowerment?[135] In Song 3:11 a woman (the groom's mother), places the crown on the head of one of Israel's great kings. Surely this is a reference to power. His mother[136] is portrayed as a "king-maker" in the way of Samuel the prophet.

The maternal motif of birthing is employed in the Song. For example in 3:4, 6:9, 8:2 and 8:5 the various terms of pregnancy and birth are used: *chaval, yalad, harah*. This power to facilitate life is often associated with the heroine's power in sexually arousing her lover. On several occasions the mother's house or boudoir becomes part of the scene. This in fact could point to the mother's womb rather than a particular building. The connotation may suggest the sexual passion of women being innate rather than learned, though the poet has the heroine exclaim that mother will "teach" her the ways of love. The wider ramifications for "motherhood" in the Song of Songs will be explored in the next chapter.

The garden theme is not the place of final consummation but it is the goal to which all parts of the Song point. Each of the prior sites is a platform from which the poet outworks the highs and lows of the journey towards the consummation of love.

Romance might be seen as particularly characterising a stage in a relationship where commitment is still not concrete. The primary motivator at this stage of a relationship is desire to know the other, but the end goal to be united, to consummate, to make their partnering permanent. Desire may be unbalanced between lovers. Love may be unrequited. These are the great and tragic risks of desire/romance/eros. Once that commitment is made, the early stages of desire and romance subside to a deeper and mature stage of monogamous, requited love.

In the garden scenes, the hero and heroine seem to play at the idea of consummation and the making of monogamous, requited and committed

---

135. In Gen 3:20 Adam describes *Chavah* (life-giver) as the mother of all living.

136. That *Shlomo's* actual mother Bat-sheva, does not seem to be relevant here. The author seems to want to emphasize the concept rather than the person.

love. The disconnection between scenes, the changing person in the discourse (i.e., movements between second and third person), the changing tense, the anachronistic movement of the scenes, provides her readers with the same frustration, angst, excitement, enchantment that the lovers themselves feel. The poet purposes the stylistic feature of discord to heighten that empathy. She persuades us that this greatest of risks is worth everything.

Reading Peshat with the Poet

This chapter has explored the discourse of the Song of Songs and shown the existence and purpose of a subtle macrostructure. Using an empathetic, author-centred reading, particular themes or sites of exploration have been further traced and oriented at the level of *peshat* (surface reading). This reading concerns itself principally with the consecutive initial progression of the poet's scenes of engagement in the text and the recognition of the orientation of the discourse on the basis of this initial progression. In my reading, the Song consistently aligns itself along seven conceptual sites (entreaty, wasf, daughters, royalty, brothers, lost and found, garden), but at many points each of these categories/locales intersects and embeds or integrates in the others in myriad ways. In line with Relevance Theory, the assumptions and presumptions/expectations of the poet have been considered selectively, highlighting various possible implications and likely effect on the reader.

The discourse analysis provides a basis upon which to explore the wider explicatures and implicatures present in the Song, particularly the text's intertextuality that must be considered further before a valid search for the deeper meaning of the Song can be expressed.

The next chapter *Remez-Derasha* will explore the allusions made in the Song that connect it to the discursive space of the Hebrew culture and worldview, the Torah and creation myth. As implied in this chapter, the Song of Songs has a provocative character and is unafraid to cross boundaries.

3

Remez-Derasha: Tracing the Contextual Environment

The Song of Songs like other biblical texts contains key words, contexts or phrases that bring to mind pictures of the past, the situations and circumstances of other biblical stories, and echoes and themes that may be found in both text and tradition. The Song is complex and the significance of these effervescent and ubiquitous motifs needs to be explored and embedded in the reading.

> I will open my mouth in parables, I will utter things hidden since the creation of the universe (Matt 13:35b NIV).[1]

The mind is very much the source of language and Relevance Theory keenly focuses on the pragmatics of the interplay between cognition and communication; "the construction of representations".[2] In the Song of Songs we are trying to reconstruct the interplay of representations that the poet sought to produce in the minds of the original audience. In ancient and pseudoepigraphic texts this is done by a forensic exploration of the text. We follow evidences in the writing that mark the contours of the poet's cognitive environment.

Stephen Pattemore suggests that capturing these contours within a text should be a priority in hermeneutics and uses Relevance Theory as a rationale. Relevance Theory views intertextuality, in particular, as crucial

---

1. From Ps 78:2
2 Sperber and Wilson, *Relevance*, 39.

evidence of the cognitive environment catalysing a text.³ The intertextuality represents key aspects of the mutual cognitive environment of the poet and audience at the time of writing. In Relevance Theory intertextuality may be categorized as weak implicature. These implicatures mark the poet's engagement of broader biblical themes or texts. This, of course, does not mean a carte blanche approach to a text where every word is a flag to another text. Relevance delimits the search for weak implicatures through the concept of optimal relevance and least-effort processing for contextual effects.

The Song of Songs goes beyond intertextuality. This song embeds herself into the traditional stories and metanarrative of the Hebrew people. The Song of Songs unfurls in the primary myths of the Hebrews. She is even iconoclastic in that she attempts and succeeds to persuade her audience to reinscribe the sacred story of origins, thereby creating an alternate; a new myth.⁴

In this chapter I combine the rabbinic hermeneutic of "echo-hunting" (*remez*) with modern sociolinguistic theory: Relevance. I find the primary Torah motif⁵ of the Garden of Eden signalled in the Song of Songs.⁶ This presents an imperative to reconnect the Song of Songs to the "Eden" text of Genesis. This rereading of the Song in the light of intertextuality with Genesis is symbolic of *derasha*.

---

3. Pattemore, "Relevance Theory," 43–60. See also Almazán García, "Dwelling in Marble Halls."

4. Eisler, *Sacred Pleasure*, 378. "Remything" in Eisler's language is to rewrite a myth in such a way that the meaning reflects the values of an enlightened society. Iconoclastic is strong language but the author does engage the story of origins in such a way. André LaCoque conceives of the Song as subversive also. LaCoque, "The Shulamite," 251.

5. In my original draft I had engaged the other motif of "the wilderness" in the Song. I continue to hold this as a significant *sitz im leben* but it will need to be explored in a subsequent writing.

6. The Song of Songs has been traditionally interpreted as a cosmic allegory of either in the Rabbinic tradition YHWH and Israel, or in the Christian tradition, God/Jesus and the church. Modern interpretations however, tend to recognize its earthy themes such as Bloch and Bloch, *The Song of Songs*, and it is often read by evangelicals as a poetic/musical anthology of love, or with an emphasis on "marital love" such as Longman, *Song of Songs*, 60. In my research I had hoped to argue for an earthy reading but found to my surprise that the Song is so replete with rich and mythic Tanakh motifs it would make a purely "earthy" reading deliberately obdurate.

Earthing the Cosmic Queen

The Garden

> I had a terrible dream, she said. You're safe, he murmured, cradling her. No, it was terrible, she said, I cannot sleep. I still see that glorious garden, the birds, the fruits, the clear streams with pebbles of agate and trancelike wandering of green fish, and you were there, and for a time it was good, but then this terrifying old man came and told me I must not think for myself. And soon a snake came and promised me and said—He laughed. A talking snake! Don't laugh, please don't laugh! She shuddered. This was so real, more real than now, much more. The snake offered me a brain and a mind and when I took them the old man came rushing in, his eyes exploding, his mouth aghast, and cursing with a hurricane force he threw us from the garden. And *you* blamed *me*, she cried, and in a world of misery we fought for five thousand years.
>
> The sun touched the window sill, touched her hair; he touched the gold along her neck and back and sighing she rolled over and for a long time they held each other, then she rose. Come see, she called, joyous beside the window. In poured the full glory of the morning, the copper-gold of sky, the far-off crowing, the clear, muted laughter along the river, the light, cool fragrance in from the fields. It will be a good day, he said, smiling. And night, she said. For years, they both thought. For years and years.[7]

The creation account of Gen 2–3 is not a happy story. It is a terribly sad story, a tragedy in fact. In a beautiful garden, a woman and a man are secluded in a world of perfect peace, fulfilled in each other, the king and queen of a private utopia. It is an eerie perfection, and so it comes as no surprise that shadows block out the light and then paradise is inevitably lost. The weakness of humankind must have lain dormant all that time and in the event of crisis, love and life was shattered.

In a complex and ornate way, Genesis evokes a poignant, profound sense of humanity's mortal condition. It is possible that in even more complex, multifaceted and ornate form, the Song of Songs rereads this ancient

---

7. A creative piece by "David" quoted in Eisler, *Sacred Pleasure*, 398–99. I don't fully sympathize with "David's" severe reading of Genesis in the poem but believe it does capture the way traditional scholarship (i.e., key theologies of the rabbinic era and early church which are based on Gen 2–3 seem to operate in a misogynist mood) on the story of origins has portrayed the Song, and it does encapsulate how women have been impacted by such readings and how the Song of Songs might in fact recover the sacred gifts intrinsic to womanhood in Scripture.

myth, as if face to face, encountering it, a terraformation. She, the poet, appears to speak of love as something that liberates the human condition from its limits, perhaps something of the divine gift of human love, sexuality and intimacy that resurrects the dead, and which, in another genre would be trampled.

The Song of Songs calls to mind the creation stories of Genesis more strongly than other pervasive scriptural motifs that might be read into the text such as the exodus or the *Golah*.[8] The Song echoes with memories of the primeval garden. Phyllis Trible in *God and the Rhetoric of Sexuality* reflects on the deep connection between the creation stories and the Song, and suggests the Song of Songs "redeems a love story gone awry."[9] And the poet of the Song does seem to, in the poet's predictably unpredictable way, audaciously recast the creation for her own incredible theology. The poet deconstructs, reconstructs, innovates, redeems and resurrects the most sacred story. Francis Landy provides a pithy synopsis of the relationship between the two texts: Paradise is lost in Genesis but "rediscovered through love" in the Song. Paradise has in fact survived in the world all this time.[10]

The poet's masterpiece, the Song of Songs, could be seen as a caveat, not a complement to the primeval aetiology of Judeo-Christianity. She seems to want to appeal for an alternate judgment by skilfully crafting a case perhaps as a cause for women, or perhaps for the primeval couple or for humanity. For this reason the similarities between the lover's world and Eden draw the reader to look to Genesis for further meaning. The contrasts between the texts become all the more significant as they suggest the poet's *crisis* (or moment) that catalyzed the text. Her *crisis* clearly concerns this broader biblical theme, or perhaps more, how her society and its laws, and its capricious freedoms have been shaped by this beloved story of origins, and how this impacts her experience of life, and freedom to love.

The Song of Songs and Genesis have clear similarities. In both texts one woman and one man are the protagonists. In both texts this man and woman are in awe of each other and sexuality is as natural and unaffected as the idyllic world around them.

---

8. While messianic and Exodus motifs are also implicit in the text, the chief focus of the poet is, as scholars like Phyllis Trible, Francis Landy, and Richard Davidson concur, the imagery and symbolism surrounding Gen 2–3, which could be realized as a hermeneutical key to the Song (Trible, "Love's Lyrics Redeemed," 144; Landy, "The Song of Songs and the Garden of Eden," 513; Davidson, *Flame of Yahweh*).

9. Trible, "Love's Lyrics," 144.

10. Landy, "The Song of Songs and the Garden of Eden," 513.

The Song clearly poses distinctions as well. In Genesis, what romance is between the primeval couple is diminished for the sake of the narrative and impending doom. In the Song, passion, love and desire are framed as the apex. There is no other purpose. The Genesis story is recounted by a narrator while in the Song of Songs the poet excludes the narrator with a furious flame. Instead the poet provides us with the *illusion of immediacy* that is the direct interaction of lovers' voices.[11] In the Song of Songs we feel the proximity and urgency of the discourse. They are ever-living (!) and near, in present tense, while the lovers of the first garden were buried in past tense long, long ago.[12]

The table below illustrates the contrasts and similarities between a selection of text from the two books, Genesis and the Song of Songs. Note the contrasting use of person. The Genesis text is clearly third person and in past tense. The narrator controls the text. God has a distinct presence. In contrast, the text from the Song of Songs is in present tense and moves intimately between first and second person. God is not a concrete presence and there is no disembodied narrator. Yet, both texts are set in scenes of nature imagery with the primary characters being a young couple.

Table 2: Comparison of Gen 2:21 and Song 7:7–12

Gen 2:21–25	Song 7:7–12
And the LORD God made Adam fall into a deep sleep, and he slept; and He took one from his ribs and closed up the flesh. And the rib which the LORD God had taken from man, made he a woman; and he brought her to the man. And Adam said, This is now bone of my bones and flesh of my flesh; and she shall be called Woman, because she was taken out of Man. Therefore shall a man leave his father and mother, and cleave to his wife; and they shall be one flesh. And they were both naked, the man and his wife, and were not ashamed.	This stature of yours is the semblance of a palm / and your breasts like its date-clusters / I said to myself "I shall ascend into this palm / I shall take hold in the crown of fronds" / Let your breasts be to me like the clusters on the vines / and you breath's fragrance like apricots / and inside your mouth like good wine / —it flows to my lover smoothly / it stirs lips from sleep / I am for my lover and upon me is his desire / . . . at daybreak we will make for the vineyards / . . . there I will give my love to you /[when] the scent of mandrakes fills the air

---

11. This "illusion of immediacy" is achieved through the deft use of "present tenses," participles, and volitionals as explored in *Peshat*.

12. Exum, "Seeing Solomon's Palanquin," 301.

Remez-Derasha: Tracing the Contextual Environment

In the following pages the contrast and likeness of the creation story and the Song of Songs is explored at a deeper level for the purpose of uncovering an impression of the crisis that may have produced the text and the theological solution that the poet seems to suggest.

Love for Love's Sake

> God said, "See, I give you every seed-bearing plant that is upon all the earth, and every tree that has seed-bearing fruit; they shall be yours for food. And to all the animals on land, to all the birds of the sky, and to everything that creeps on earth, in which there is the breath of life, [I give] all the green plants for food." And it was so (Gen 1:29–30).

Understanding the society in which the poet and audience lived is vital to understanding the mutual cognitive environment in which a text is born. Carol Meyers sets Gen 2–3 against the valid and significant backdrop of pioneering Israel, the presumed original audience.[13] Meyer's data suggests that the living conditions of the early years in Canaan were incredibly difficult for the Hebrews. Death rates from studies of burial groups show that up to 35% of the population died in infancy, and up to 50% died before the age of 18. Women often died before the age of 30 due to the heavy childbearing demands, while men might survive to the age of 40. It was not uncommon for disease to routinely devastate these frontier villages according to archaeological findings. In contrast to the likely reality, the creation garden is beyond idyllic.

Although the *Sitz im Leben* of the Song of Songs is probably the civilized and established Judah rather than the daunting period of the pioneers, the harsh realities of family life continued in this period. Women bear many children and those famed "gazelle" breasts and wheat pile stomachs belong to a brief period of adolesence. The ravages of disease and age mean fragrant mouths and non-"bereaved" teeth are unlikely to exist for more than a short youthful season.[14]

---

13. The late Bronze, early Iron age. Meyers, *Discovering Eve*, 50ff.

14. Carey Walsh provides an entertaining description of the toiletry habits of a typical couple in the period of the Song in her exploration of "breath of apricots." Walsh, *Exquisite Desire*, 101.

> Enjoy life with the wife you have loved throughout your meaningless life that he has given you under the sun, all the days of your futility; for that is your allotted portion in life and in your labor that you work at under the sun (Eccl 9:9).

Given the reality of life in the ancient world according to Meyers and Walsh, the private world of the young man and woman of the Song of Songs is as uncomplicated as Eden in many ways. There is no hard working of the ground, no pregnancy and no associated responsibilities of child bearing and rearing.[15] They seem emancipated from both male and female gendered roles in labor in the snapshots we are provided by the poet. In their private world of *shalom* (i.e., the garden scenes) there are no social structures, no enemies, no threats, no constraints and no mention of marriage. These two are for each other and everything is wonderful when they are together in these exclusive and exotic locales. The poet applies no fault to their togetherness. They love for love's sake alone. Their world is bountiful and benevolent. But the reality of the world outside theirs contrasts their world of love dramatically at times. The lovers regularly endure an outside world that is fraught with social responsibilities and expectations, enemies, "others," threats and constraints. In their private and utopian world their only support is from "friends," benevolent insiders who appear overtly only twice in the Song (5:1, 8:13). The benevolent insider is perhaps by the poet's design located in the gentle reader—the audience, ourselves—those the poet persuades to value the couple's star-crossed love. The first audiences and even today's reader become "friends" or comrades if they feast and drink with the lovers and listen for their voice.

The two lovers in the Song are as one with the created world of *chayot* [animals], just like the primal couple in Genesis, however not quite in the same sense. That is, there is no rule or dominion over nature for the lovers. They seem to fuse with the natural world without leaving a trace. If there is dominion or rule, it is not visible. No violence transpires in the Song's garden.[16] There is beneficial interplay with even wild and dangerous animals. All creatures perform compassionate roles in the story of passion. Leopards, lions, wild stags, gazelles, sheep, goats and nightingale, the doves,

---

15. Please see the discourse analysis, level 7, *the Garden*. The world of the garden is, as I have noted, a utopia.

16. Note also the absence of eating "meat" *basar* in the Song. It seems that no animal is killed in this production (though jackals are seized). Once again this points to the Garden of Eden where the diet was vegetarian; where there is no death except in the refusal to love. See also Brenner, "The Food of Love," 105.

all contribute to the idyllic garden setting and work only to accentuate the loveliness of this other world. In the Song the poet represents such a deep reconnection with the world of creation that animal images and animal metaphors merge even in the lover's descriptions of each other (Song 2:9, 14; 4:1, 2, 5; 6:5, 6).

> The Song is a reflection on the story of the Garden of Eden, using the same images of garden and tree, substituting for the traumatic dissociation of man and animals their metaphoric integration. Through this glimpse, belatedly, by the grace of poetry, is the possibility of paradise.[17]

The same is true with the botanical world. The images of plants, organic perfumes and resins overlap into images of the lovers themselves. They drip with myrrh, aloes and honey. The lovers are decorated with herbage (Song 1:14; 7:2), their mouths are like lotus (5:13); the heroine describes herself as a wildflower (2:1), he is like a fruit-tree (2:3), she a date palm (7:7) and an entire orchard of pomegranates (4:13). The imagery of plant life as with animal life is so integrated with the lovers that it is impossible to neatly separate them. The poet's poetic genius allows the reader to re-embrace the creation story through this contemporary tale of love, and almost hear the refrain echo from Genesis 1:10: . . . *and God saw it and it was good.*

LIBERATING THE FEMININE

The poet may have a subtle agenda in the Song of Songs that seeks to liberate womanhood from her indictment in Eden.[18] Much has been written against women from a theological viewpoint in the history of Jewish and

---

17. Landy, "The Song of Songs," 318.

18. The liberation the masculine in the Song is not so easily argued as is the feminine. I would like to argue a strong liberation of the masculine but the evidence for such an argument is not substantial. The panegyric throughout the Song by the heroine sometimes starkly contrasts with the hero's actions. In contrast to the heroine his search for the heroine is less successful (5:6, 8:14), and his part in their love, in contrast, seems to cost less in risk or effort is concerned (1:7b, 3:2, 5:7), the stakes not quite so high. His speech such as that in Song 1:8 seem to query his genuine concern. He has far greater freedom of movement, i.e., Song 2:8, but is more often than not, not to be found (1:7, 5:8). There is a small window of opportunity where the use of Gen 1–3 may allow a reading of certain portions of the Song in favour of a redemption of Eden's man. I discuss this in the section "Restoring Man" below.

Christian traditions.[19] The shards of this shattered love between women and men have littered the world since the tale of origins was first spun, at that moment when Adam uttered, *The woman, whom you gave to be with me*, and the then dreadful words of God to the woman in response, *What is this that you have done?* (Gen 3:11b–13b).

Landy paints a similar picture of the tried and tested but now triumphant woman of the Song:

> Metaphorically aligned with a feminine aspect of divinity, associated with the celestial bodies, the land, and fertility, the Beloved reversed the predominantly patriarchal theology of the Bible. Male political power is enthralled to her . . .[20]

The woman is proactive in the original garden. It is she who discovers, speaks and chooses, and eats and leads the man to eat, but the text of Genesis is devastating and the narrator merciless. In Genesis 3:13 she is condemned for her actions and Adam for his inaction and they are sent broken from their perfect garden and locked out forever; a fire breathing cherub barring the way (Gen 3:24).

Not so in the Song of Songs. The text radiates the aura of the poet's approbation. Implicitly the heroine is commended for her actions: she speaks wisdom (2:7; 3:5), she runs (1:4), leads (8:2), kisses (1:2), embraces (2:6; 8:3), calls (5:6) and eats (2:3), all without judgment. She is not misguided, deceived, naïve, unsure (Gen 3:13b). In this writing she is wonderful, more brilliant than the dawn, more awesome than the constellations, a "well of living waters" (4:15):

> . . . descend to me from Lebanon
> From this snowclad peak come down
> Look down from the summit of Amarna
> From the peaks of Senir and Hermon . . . (Song 4:8).

---

19. Riane Eisler goes to great lengths in her book, *Sacred Pleasure*, 72–160, to review the history of the domination of women and in parts writes persuasively with regards to the growth of monotheism and subsequent suppression of women.

20. Landy goes on eloquently, "The lovers live, however, in a patriarchal world; the Beloved suffers the humiliation that attends sexually adventurous women. She is cast out of her family (1:6), despised by Shepherds (1:7), beaten by watchmen (5:7). The lovers can only find or imagine an enclosure, secluded from the world: a garden, a forest bed, or the poem itself. The poem is unfailingly critical of a world that does not know the true value of love and that imposes shame on lovers . . ." (Landy, "The Song of Songs," 316).

Remez-Derasha: Tracing the Contextual Environment

She has transcended and appears like a heavenly being. She comes down from sacred peaks. She appears *like the morning star.*[21]

She is a warrior queen (7:4). She is strong and brave, fearless, resolute (3:2). Her qualities are compared to the fearless men of old, armed and established in a stone fortress (4:4). She carries no sword and no shield, but risks all on her own particular battlefield (5:7). She is braver than the warriors who hold swords to their sides "against the fears of the night" (3:8). She has no fear of the night and has twice demonstrated her willingness to challenge the darkness (3:1ff. and 5:2ff.).

In implicit contrast to Genesis 3 her gift of speech is celebrated. Her speech in the Song is lovely, pleasant (2:14, 4:3). Her speech is core to the text. Her voice opens the Song and is the last to trail away.[22] There is no indictment here. She hasn't said too much. Her hero longs for her to speak, to share her intimate thoughts and words, "Let me hear your voice!" he exclaims (Song 2:14). He calls her "friend."[23]

This emphasis on voice is strongly linked to *gan' eden*. The couple's voices and words are a focal point. Like God's creative speech, these two create their own paradise, name their world and establish linguistic boundaries between themselves and the trampling of the outside world, all through words, *whatever Adam called every living creature, that was its name* (Gen 2:19–20a).

In the original garden, Adam was given the task to name his world, but in the Garden of Eden the narrator seems to imply that the entire exercise of naming was to prove one thing: there was not a thing in the world that could truly bring him wholeness except that of a human *other*. In the Song the poet has the couple together, finding delight in naming their private world innovating on yet another of the primeval divine gifts.

Love and Death

It is perhaps the domain in which the poet empowers her heroine. It is an existential domain; that of life and death, and in which she reaches the very heights of life. This domain of life is also the domain of eroticism and

---

21. She is a "daughter of the dawn" (compare Isa 14:12).

22. Trible, "Love's Lyrics," 145.

23. The heroine's voice is applauded overtly in 2:14 and 8:13. She is commonly referred to as "friend" or "companion" by the hero in 1:2, 15; 2:2 and another six occasions.

love not available to the world of uncompassionate outsiders.[24] It is from this sanctuary of abundant life, that the Song of Songs reaches a number of summits where the heroine of the text achieves a kind of actualization, such as that in Song 8:6–7. This intense, raw and memorable lacuna in the text provokes the theology of Gen 1–3 in a startling way. In Gen 2:17 death was introduced as the punishment the primeval couple would bring upon themselves if they ate from that tree. In Genesis 3, the woman's decision to eat, and the man's decision to follow her and then indict her, resulted in brokenness, and death came into the world. Death in the text thus becomes the status quo of human experience—the last gate through which all living must pass. However, the poet has the heroine of the Song of Songs confront death openly. Her love is primordial Death's worthy opponent, Song 8:6–7:

> Set me as a seal upon your heart
> A seal on your arm
> For love is as vehement as death
> Its passion as relentless as sheol
> A radiant flaming fire
> Oceans cannot overwhelm love
> Surging rivers cannot drown it out . . .

This woman's love challenges the death ordained in Gen 2:17. Her love will remain even after the assuaging of the primeval waters of chaos and the final closing of the eyes. Her love redeems. But this love is also terrifying and paradoxical. Francis Landy explores this tension in *Beauty and the Enigma*.[25] Such love, such integration can swallow up the participants as in the scene 1:12–13 where both the hero and heroine lose definition and individuality as they become scent, night, warmth and then oblivion—and yet more the essence of life and humanity than either has been before. The lover collapses into the other and both lose "self" in their unification but gain the cosmos. The climax of love-making is thus aptly named, *le petit mort*.

---

24. Trible, "Love's Lyrics," 145.
25. Landy, *Beauty and the Enigma*, 35–95.

Woman as Garden

> Awake Zaphon! Come Tayman!
> Breathe into my garden
> Let my perfumes escape
> Let my lover come into his garden
> And taste its treasure of fruit . . . (Song 4:16).

While *garden* in the Song is a geographical space in that both lovers may actually go there, this metaphor fuses into imagery that associates the garden with the heroine, the heroine's body. She is not the foolish woman who ruins the Narrator's primeval garden with her desire. She is the garden in the text of the Song. She is paradise in the eyes of her hero.

According to Walsh, the poet's correlation of the heroine with the garden is a logical and spatial connection considering what gardens meant in Israel.[26] Gardens were situated close to the home on the terraced hillsides. The farmer on coming home from the field would ascend through the garden on his way to his house, and descend into it from his home. It was connected with the woman of the home in two ways. She worked in the home and close to the garden. She would be more likely to tend the garden as part of her labors around the home. The pleasures of eating a piece of water-laden fruit on returning home from the sun in the dry field "enhances the ancient farmer's quality of life" and the associated sweet pleasures of loving his woman are not difficult to connect as intersecting images.[27]

> Into the grove of walnuts I descended
> To see the lushness of the streams
> To see the budding vines
> The red-bursting flowers of the pomegranate trees
> (Song 6:11)

Walsh goes further in her descriptions of garden imagery and focuses on the nature of keeping vines.[28] She sees in the keeping of vines clearly the heated sexuality of the lovers. The poet of the Song of Songs clearly represents the vineyard as a metaphor for a woman. The woman of the Song, speaking of herself claims she has not kept her vineyard (1:6) and then at last that her vineyard is her own (8:12). Yet the vineyard is also a place where both lovers may journey and love.

---

26. Walsh, *Exquisite Desire*, 116.
27. Ibid.
28. Ibid., 129–34.

> At daybreak we'll make for the vineyards
> We'll see if the vines are budding with open blossoms
> ... There I will give you my love
> When the scent of mandrakes fills the air (Song 7:12–13)

Walsh explains that "darkened grapes hang heavily on the vine, engorged with juice, and in triangular clusters. Women would be harvesting these fruits, cementing an association."[29] But even further than this, Walsh believes the association of the heroine and the vineyard well describes an aroused woman. The juice of grapes is prized and made into wines that are intoxicating when drunk deeply. Apart from the "innocently provocative" appearance of ripe grapes, the tending of grapes requires skilled cultivation to produce a maximum ripening and harvest. The oral delight of grapes and their wines and requirement for dexterous handiwork on the part of the vintner provides ample metaphor for sexuality. Walsh goes even further.

> The vintner/lover has to bother to get to know what the woman wants and what arouses her. And astonishingly in this Song, he comes to even appreciate her arousal *as an end in itself,* one that eclipses any goal of penetration or procreation![30]

This is certainly an unlikely concept to be central to the contextual environment of the priestly redactors of Gen 2–3, as Walsh implies, but concepts like this are very much within the range of interest for the poet.[31]

> [O woman] dweller-in-gardens. . . .
> Our comrades listen for your voice!

As a capstone, the poet of the Song of Songs has the heroine as garden-dweller in the final lines, Song 8:13. It is a longed-for avowal of the Feminine in relation to the Garden, a liberation from the captivity of the "original sin" brought about by the poet's persuasive and tenacious emphasis on her belonging. The poet turns the metaphor every possible way. The woman is in the garden, seeks the garden and becomes the garden. As the Song fades away, this woman finds her home in the very garden from which she was originally humiliated and cast.

---

29. Ibid., 130.
30. Ibid., 90, 132.
31. Ibid., 105ff. Walsh quips, "The woman in this Song is fruitful in ways the Priestly writer never could have dreamed."

Liberating Desire and Eating Fruit

It was the desire of the woman in the first garden that was implicitly condemned. In Genesis 3:6 the narrator relays the thought processes of the woman:

> When the woman saw that the tree was good for food, that it had a pleasing appearance and that the tree was desirable for making one wise, she took some of its fruit and ate (Gen 3:6).

In the Song of Songs the actual eating of fruit merges with metaphor as fruit becomes symbolically love, but also sexuality. Fruit presents a synaesthesia of the physical, erotic aspects of love-making, but also the quality and timbre of the young couple's love, and the lovers themselves. In the words of Gordis, "the language of symbolism . . . is superior [to allegory] because its elements possess both existential reality and a representational character of their own."[32] This symbolism of fruit in the Song deftly communicates the lovers' delicacy in their treatment of each other, their mutual satisfaction, their sufficiency for each other, their yearning, and the holistic-ripeness of their experience of love. Francis Landy notes that most of the images including fruit and the lovers themselves in the Song "participate in a number of paradigms," connecting and reconnecting in multiple ways.[33]

It was the great desire for a beautiful fruit that led to the downfall of the primeval couple. In the Song of Songs the poet goes too far so wonderfully. Fruit is absolutely ubiquitous in the Song. There is a riot of fruit consumption and much more than just a few bites. The fruit of the lovers' garden is tasted, sampled and sucked: *Let my lover come into his garden and taste its treasures of fruit* (4:16); rolled about in the mouth: *his fruit is sweet in my mouth*, (2:3); dripped, oozed, savoured and drunk (4:11; 5:1, 13; 7:9). The lovers look like fruit: *your cheek like a pomegranate* (4:3). They breathe fruit: *your breath is like apricots* (7:8). Fruit is even lain in: *let me rest with caked-raisins, lay me down with apricots* (2:5). The heroine becomes an entire grove of fruit trees: *you branch out like a grove of fruiting pomegranates* (4:13) and the hero also, *like a fruiting apricot among the woodland trees* (2:3). There are apricots, pomegranates, figs, walnuts, dates, raisons, grapes, and all their accompanying preserves, wines, juices and syrups. These species are at once concrete and metaphor as they represent often the bodies of

---

32. Gordis, *The Song of Songs*, 32.
33. Landy, "The Song of Songs and the Garden of Eden," 515.

the heroine and the hero. There is a hyperbolic smorgasbord of fruit in the Song and with it the poet seems determined to challenge the circumstances of Genesis 3:

> When the woman saw that the tree was good for food, that it had a pleasing appearance and that the tree was desirable for making one wise, she took some of its fruit and ate. She also gave some to her husband, who was with her; and he ate. Then the eyes of both of them were opened (Gen 3:6–7a).

There is fruit here from what appears to be that sacred tree, because the qualities of this fruit are that of opening eyes and awakening.[34] In contrast to the Eden story, this fruit brings life not death, saves not destroys, and the lovers are encouraged to feast (4:16, 5:1).

The negative desire of Genesis is further encumbered by the "curse" of Genesis 3:16, and God's action is strike her womb and her desire, *Yet to your husband will be your teshuqa [desire] and he will overrule you.*

Now the woman will be caught in a net of domination by her desire forever more. However in the Song of Songs even this reality experienced by so many women is engaged and reversed. Using the same language, *teshuqa*, the Song's heroine claims in Song 7:10: *I am for my lover and his teshuqa [desire] is upon me.*

In the Song of Songs' alternate universe, mutual desire and belonging, not overruling, is the status quo. The "divinely-ordained" dominion of patriarchy is cracked. The Song's new relational ethic redeems a world of pain. The lovers heal each other, protect each other, embrace each other, revel in the other's otherness and empower each other.

Further in Genesis, *teshuqa* again holds a negative connotation. This time the son of the woman is warned about sin. Sin is described as "crouching at the door": *It wants [teshuqah] you, but you can rule over it* (Gen 4:7).

Here with further clarity *desire* is associated with negative imagery and repeats the refrain of Genesis 3:16 directed at the woman. The poet of the Song could not be more brazen in her engagement and liberation of desire. What is in creation firstly a feminine trait, a dangerous weakness, and further associated with sinfulness, is in the Song of Songs, the heroine's

---

34. Fruit invariably appears in the scenes of love (in *the Garden*) which are episodes framed by terms like rouse, awaken, stir up in the troths (2:7, 3:5) but consider also the sense of *behold* in 3:11 and in 5:2, *I sleep but my heart is awake* as evidence for feasting on the fruit of love as awakening and enlightening, and that perhaps the mood of the Song supports that without love, it is no life at all (i.e., 8:6–7).

Remez-Derasha: Tracing the Contextual Environment

strength and salvation. It is her desire that leads her to the peak of human existence; her desire leads her to drink from the fountain of life.

Liberating the Masculine

There is also a liberation of the masculine in the Song of Songs. The hero's careful tending of his garden-woman in the poet's eyes, fulfils one of the ideals of Genesis, that of tending and tilling the Garden (Gen 2:15).

The poet has the hero descend twice into the garden in a way reminiscent of God himself in Gen 2:7 and 19 and, especially 3:8-9, when he descends to walk in the original garden in the cool of the evening, and when God called out, *Where are you?*[35]

Compare the text from the Song (6:2).

> My lover descended into his garden
> [Through] terraces of balsam
> To shepherd in the gardens
> And harvest the lotus . . .

And again in 6:11–12 as the hero speaks in first person:

> Into the grove of walnuts I descended
> To see the lushness of the streams
> To see the budding vines
> The blossoming pomegranates . . .

There is a care and focus for the man in these passages that does much to recover his potency that was lacking in the creation saga. It seems in this man is so much the true image of *Elohim*, (Imago Dei), that he is in this text, perhaps finally, the authentic representation.

Image of God and the Garden-Temple

The Genesis concept of humankind made in the image of *Elohim*, Imago Dei, allows some of the deistic language in the Song, particularly the ornate language of Gen 1:27: *So God created man in His own image; in the image of God created he him: male and female He created them.*

The phrasing and vocabulary of Genesis implies that at least part if not all of creation was an architectural work for the purpose of building a

---

35. Also the many instances in Torah, e.g., Gen 11:5; Exod 3:8; 19:20.

temple-palace for God.³⁶ For example the creation is hammered out (such as the firmament in Gen 1:3, *raqiyah*) and elsewhere in scripture this motif is drawn upon to describe the work of creation (such as Job 38:4–38) where the poet has God speak explicitly and at length of the "building" or "construction" of creation.

Once the Temple-Palace is built, the image of the god is displayed. There is evidence to support this temple-garden concept in Gen 1:26–27, when man and woman are created in the image of God. In the ANE the king is considered the premier "Image of god" (and really the only significant god-image; living god). In this, the Hebrew creation myth exhibits a radical element because the implication of the text of Gen 1:27 is that everyman and everywoman, not just the King, is somehow inherently a living god.³⁷

In chapters 5 and 7 the poet has constructed two *wasf* almost mirroring each other with regard to content and structure. The interesting and startling thing concerning these two *wasf* is their comparison of the lovers to what can only be described as the stone gods of the type worshipped all over the ANE in temples, and also carried by palanquin through the streets of cities. By comparing the lovers to idols, the poet now skirts close to the razor edge of the Decalogue (Exod 20:3): *You are not to make for yourselves a carved image.*³⁸

> His hands are wheels of gold
> Filled in with sea-green chrysoprase [*tarshish*-stone]
> The seat of his manhood carved ivory
> Encrusted with lapis lazuli (5:14)

The phrase that connects "wheels" with "tarshish-stone" evokes Ezekial 1:16: *As for the appearance and structure of the wheels, they gleamed like beryl* [*tarshish*-stone].

Both stones mentioned in Song 5:14 also conjure up Ezekiel's prophetic word to the King of Tzor. In this scripture the garden, the stones and beauty/perfection are connected. Literally these precious stones and metals are moulded, worked and set into this image of the King: *You were in Eden, the garden of God; Every precious stone was your adornment* (Ezek 28:12–13).

---

36. Watts, "Making Sense of Genesis."
37. Ibid.
38. The author's "dalliance" with idols seems to trivialize a most sacred *mitzvah*. The question is one of purpose in doing such a thing. The answer must lie in the garden which transcends Mosaic law—the garden has precedent over Moses.

Remez-Derasha: Tracing the Contextual Environment

Ezekiel reveals a precedent for the integrating of Eden imagery into the texts of the culture. This imagery was a time-honored pillar in the culture's discursive space. Even if the contexts and chronologies vastly differ in the Song, this precedent substantiates the reading of Song 5:10–16 as language describing statues of gods.

In the Song, the earthiness of the lover is imbued by the transcendent and sacred. He becomes Imago Dei, the new Adam.

Othmar Keel notes that the statues of gods were constructed of these kinds of materials. In Egypt the blue stones represented the "ocean of heaven" (sky) or the primal ocean from which the god rises. The gold represents the light of the sun and stars. In a twentieth century (BCE) hymn to the son of the sun-god in Thebes the Pharaoh is described thus: *His limbs were inlaid with gold, his head-covering was lapis lazuli . . .*[39]

The imagery of our hero as a stone god grows in Song 5:15: *His thighs alabaster pillars / His calves [establish themselves on] pedestals of fine gold.* Buoyed by the reference to Eden and the King of Tzor in Ezekiel we have an "image of god" in the garden. From comparative literature, Othmar Keel invokes *Medinet Habu*, composed by Pharaoh's daughter:

> Your hair is lapis lazuli,
> Your eyebrows are *qa'*-stone,
> Your eyes green malachite,
> Your mouth is red jasper.[40]

Like the mirror image of her lover, the heroine is illustrated as a statue of a goddess in Song 7:2b-3.

> The joints of your thighs are jewelled
> The handiwork of an artisan
> Your "navel" is as a hammered basin
> That mulled wine never ebbs
> Your belly a dome of wheat
> Encircled by lotus

Othmar Keel's commentary contains drawings of Sumerian goddess figurines with a single round disk over their lower abdomen.[41]

The poet here deifies the young lovers; creates images of them that cannot help but lead to a representation based on stone gods. But once

---

39. Keel, *The Song of Songs*, 202.
40. Ibid., 203.
41. Ibid., 232.

again the answer to the poet's seemingly idolatrous implications make sense if the creation texts of Genesis are invoked. The poet seems to draw the reader back to the beginning, reminding the reader that love transcends the contemporary religious dogma (of the primary audience's day) and thus perhaps defies the male-dominated ritual of the Temple.[42] The concept of Imago Dei in the Song could support a bold application of Gen 1:27 into the poet's contemporary situation. The poet proposes a precedent prior to Moses. As was in the garden, "You are gods."[43]

One Flesh

> Therefore shall a man leave his father and his mother and shall cleave to his wife; and they shall be one flesh (Gen 2:24).

The way in which the Song of Songs leaps and skips between vignettes, scenes and scenarios, sometimes with disorienting effect, is often used to support an anthology of poems rather than a single poem. In contrast, the numerous correlations and intersecting images and threads suggest an organic wholeness. The Song of Songs is, in short, an enigma at even the structural level.

For an example of discordance in the Song of Songs, the two correlating *wasfs* of the hero and the heroine featured in the above section occur non-consecutively in the Song (ch. 5 and 7). But discordance and concordance can also exist within the same lines. These same *wasfs* provide a balance in the Song at a deeper level. The heroine makes conflicting claims regarding *her* vineyard in 1:6 and 8:12 but these also seem to form a macro-inclusio around the Song that suggests actualization in the heroine's perception of her identity. There are four similar adjurations for the *banot Yerushalaim* punctuating the Song sporadically and yet consolidating it. The random yet consistent changes of person, the seemingly arbitrary and capricious movements of scene and scenario are further indications of the predictable unpredictability of the Song.

There is the oddly correlating yet disorienting occurrence of two night-time scenes in chapters 3 and 5. These are similar stories with alternate

---

42. Richard Davidson believes that the fertility cults are also denounced and transcended by this deep valuing of the human other. Davidson, *Flame of Yahweh*, 84ff., 554ff.

43. As a later prophet would also aver, that through love his body would transcend the temple and death itself. Ps 82:6; John 10:34.

Remez-Derasha: Tracing the Contextual Environment

endings: one triumphant, one tragic. There are the arbitrary appearances of *Shlomo* in the Song. Sometimes he is a hero as on his wedding day in chapter 3, and sometimes a fool: the owner of *Ba'al Hamon* in chapter 8. One would expect an organic text to move towards a final climax, but the Song of Songs is punctuated with climaxes and anti-climaxes. Even in the last lines of the text the hero and heroine are still separated. There is no finale, no ultimate consummation.

> This concluding scene suggests the status of the poem; the discourse of the lovers separates them. It is a displacement of love, in which foreplay—seduction, sweet-talk—repeatedly defers fusion.[44]

There appears to be purposefulness to the disconnection and unpredictable progressions in the content and macrostructure particularly if the poet's work on the Song is presumed to be genius rather than carelessness.[45] I concur with Landy in that the Song of Songs' macrostructure is the poet's intent to engage at yet a further level the eternal male-female struggle to be bone of bone, flesh of flesh, *one flesh*.

> The union of lovers through metaphor, their discovery of correlates, and of themselves, in and through each other, is the poetic process. The poem is integrated as the lovers are integrated; through its work all the fragments of the world cohere, and are granted significance in a single vision . . . [but the poetic process is also evidenced] . . . in the violence with which it dismembers the body, its total disregard for logical connection, the abruptness with which it embarks upon and abandons episodes in the lives of the lovers. The disunity is also that of the lovers, whose work of integration can never be completed. Constantly they assert differences and distances. One is a [lotus], the other is an [apricot] tree; one is a roe, the other a dove . . .[46]

The poet writes twice in the text of perfection. It would be ironic for such a focus on the flawlessness of someone loved (as in Song 4:7) to be represented by an inept arrangement of discontinuous poetry. Once again the poet distances herself from outsiders.[47] The poet seems to allow for the

---

44. Landy, "The Song of Songs," 316.

45. Walsh describes this feature as, "embodying the very emotion it is describing." Walsh, *Exquisite Desire*, 28.

46. Landy, "The Song of Songs," 316.

47. Such critical readers were found in the Qumran sect who discarded erotic portions of the Song for reasons of its excessive prurience, see earlier discussion. But note

suspicious reader to see the text as flawed, reflecting this suspicion as if the text was a mirror. The reader may well find himself uncovered. But Shulamith who is also the Garden, is also the Song. The purposed flaw of discontinuity could also be the poet's coup de grâce. Song 4:7, 6:9:

> Everything about you is beautiful, my love
> You are without a flaw . . .
> My dove, my perfect one, is unique
> Her mother's only child
> The darling of the one who bore her . . .

The poet's text is beautiful, artful and surprising. It seems that rather, the Song of Songs has been written to illustrate deeply the miracle of human sexuality and illustrate this at multiple levels. In this light, the disjointedness found in the Song could be seen to demonstrate further the dichotomy of two individuals seeking to become one flesh.

> The germinal paradox of the Song is the union of two people through love. The lovers search for each other through the world and through language that separates them and enfolds them.[48]

Francis Landy goes further to illustrate that within the language of the Song the punctuated representation of duality: two roes, two breasts, two lips, and even quite obscure phrases like *split pomegranate* and the contrasting of colors, white and red, signifies an ornate return to Gen 2:24, of cleaving and joining. On both macro and micro-scale the poet has perfected the Song.

Sleeping and Awaking

The poet orients her song between reality and dream. The fragmented quality of the Song of Songs has sometimes been described as the poet's dreams within dreams.[49]

---

also Sigmund Freud cited in André LaCocque "[There are] various methods . . . for making [an undesirable] book innocuous. [1] Offending passages . . . [can be] made illegible . . . The next copyist would produce a text . . . which had gaps. [2] Another way would be . . . to proceed to distort the text. [3] Best of all, the whole passage would be erased and a new one which said exactly the opposite put in its place" (LaCocque, "The Shulamite," 235).

48. Landy, "The Song of Songs," 305.
49. Keel, *The Song of Songs*, 119.

Remez-Derasha: Tracing the Contextual Environment

Sleeping and waking is of course significant in the stories of origins in Genesis. When Adam discovers through his zoological study (Gen 2:19) that he is in fact alone he falls [*naphal*] into a deep sleep [*tardemah*]:

> So the LORD God cast a deep sleep upon the man; and, while he slept, He took one of his ribs, and closed up the flesh at that spot. And the LORD God fashioned the rib that he had taken from the man into a woman; and He brought her to the man (Gen 2:21–22).

When the man awoke, he awoke to an epiphany, which the narrator interrupts in order to better express by poetry how things are, beginning: *This one at last / Is bone of my bones / And flesh of my flesh . . .* (Gen 2:23–24).

There are many instances in the Song of Songs at the level of content where the poet engages with concepts of sleep and waking. Imagery and vocabulary that suggest sleep appear early in the Song whereas wakefulness, consciousness, arousal tends to appear more frequently in the second half of the Song. The two concepts overlap even in the same lines. The phrase: *swear to me . . . never to arouse and awaken love until desire is full*, (Song 2:7, 3:5, 8:4) that is thrice refrained in the Song asks for a promise to never awaken, to continue to slumber. There is tension between the two and the promise invoked serves only to foreground the possibility of awakening to eros. There is a sense that it would be a travesty not to awaken, given the Song itself is given over to celebrating desire. Perhaps it is safer to slumber. The heroine is set on a course to full arousal. Her desire is full to the brim. She is determined to experience life's heights, willing also to pay the great cost.

The following figure shows many such instances, where the poet implies both waking and sleep in the Song of Songs. Many of the scenarios of sleep suggest darkness or night. The imagery of sleep can be both restful and secure. A metamorphosis occurs during sleep. But the poet also hints at the dark and the terrible aspects of sleep. Some scenarios are nightmarish.

Images of sleep
- ... where will you let them rest in the heat of noon (1:7)
- ...As the king reclines, my musk-scented nard, its fragrance breathes/ .... between my breasts he rests through the night... (1:12)
- our bed is lush, green grass... (1:16)
- let me rest with caked raisons, lay me down with apricots... (2:5)
- never arouse nor awaken love (2:7)
- shadows of night (2:17)
- on my bed by night I yearned... (3:1)
- never awaken love (3:5)
- against the fears of the night (3:8)
- shadows of night (4:6)
- descend to me (4:8)
- I sleep but my heart is awake... (5:2)
- my lover descended into his garden (6:2)
- into the garden of walnuts I descended (6:11)
- its stirs lips that sleep (7:10)
- lets pass the night among the henna (7:12)
- never awaken love (8:4)
- then I was in his eyes as one who has found peace (8:10)

Images of waking
- awaken when desire is full (2:7)
- Rise up and come (2:10)
- rise up and come (2:13)
- until day breathes (2:17)
- I must arise... ascend (3:2)
- the one who birthed me (3:4)
- awaken when desire is full (3:5)
- arise daughters... behold ... (3:11)
- until day breathes (4:6)
- you have quickened me (4:9)
- you branch out *[shalach]* (4:13)
- awake Zaphon! (4:16)
- my heart is awake (5:2)
- arise and open (5:5)
- ... the one who birthed her (6:9)
- I descended to see ... to see... (6:11)
- I did not know my passion/ it set me in chariots (6:12)
- at daybreak we will... see (7:13)
- she will teach me (8):2
- awaken when desire is full (8:4)
- beneath the apricot tree I awoke you. there your mother birthed you (8:5)

Figure 5: Images/hints of sleep and waking in the Song of Songs

In the Song the imagery of wakefulness balances sleep. At one end of the conceptual range of *wakefulness* characters display perceptivity, spiritual alertness and what might be described as transcendent consciousness (such as the lovers' discourses). Some characters also seem caricatured as looking but not perceiving, that is, trapped in sleep and never fully waking.[50] On occasion the daughters of Jerusalem fall into this category (5:9), as do the voyeurs of the *Shulamith*'s dance in Song 7:1–2. The poet portrays these outsiders as staring, as if in a trance, or a dream, as if not awake to the actuality of the dancer's love. The *Shulamith* is degraded by their objectifying gaze and their demands for her to dance. At the king's wedding in chapter 3 the daughters of Jerusalem are granted a new title daughters of Zion [*banot Zion*] (3:9) which accompanies their *arising and beholding* in a way that suggests a deepening of their consciousness, signalled further by this new appellation. The exact reason for their rise in status in the eyes of the poet is

---

50. Rather like the scenario in Isaiah 6:9ff where the Hebrews are rebuffed by the prophet for seeing not perceiving and listening but not hearing.

Remez-Derasha: Tracing the Contextual Environment

cryptic. They look at a king's joy in his marriage. They see his mother crown him. The poet may intend to contrast this *beholding* of the women to the *staring* men at the dance (6:13; 7:1). It seems that the daughters of Zion understood something profound in the scene, especially with the appearance of the Queen-mother who guides the event. Perhaps other less "awakened" courtiers may have only seen a powerful man acquiring a possession.

Dressing and Undressing

In the Garden of Eden, when Adam awakes to discover he is no longer alone, but has a companion—a woman—who is the answer to his heart's cry, the narrator makes the following revelation: *And they were both naked, the man and his wife, and were not ashamed* (Gen 2:25).

There is an innocence attributed to the man and woman in the garden at this point. They moved before each other without self-consciousness. They encountered each other with the innocence of children. It is not clear here whether the couple found each other erotic as such, and no concrete evidence of a sexual dimension to their relationship.[51] Eroticism is a gradual uncovering which prioritizes the art or beauty of the subject, evoking an emotional and aroused response in the viewer—that is, the desire for what is beyond the veil. Pornography on the other hand is the coarse display of objects that prioritizes domination, subjection and control.[52]

In the climax of the primeval couple's story their consciousness of their own bodies undergoes a terrible change in Gen 3:7–11, they discover shame in their nakedness: *They heard the sound of the LORD God moving about in the garden at the [cool] of the day; and the man and his wife hid from the LORD God.*

The poet provides in the Song, beautiful episodes of rediscovery of the male and female body without the shamefulness ascribed to such an uncovering in the Garden of Eden after eating from the tree. The poet does this delicately through erotic metaphor. Through the soft veil of metaphor the celebration of skin is clear. The lovers uncover and celebrate each other's body layer by layer and from head to foot.

---

51. The narrator explicitly states that Adam *knew* his wife in Gen 4:1 after the tragedy of Gen 3.

52. Walsh, *Exquisite Desire*, 44–45.

> My lover is dazzling white and wine-red
> He stands like a banner . . .
> His head shines pure gold
> His thick mane raven-black
> His eyes . . .
> His cheeks . . .
> His mouth . . .
> His arms . . .
> His loins . . . (5:10–16).

The poet does not completely recover for the lovers the innocence and emancipation of the first days of Eden. The heroine suffers humiliation at the hands of society particularly when abused by the watchmen in Song 5:7. She still feels shame when she rejects the thought of appearing "like a veiled one" by the shepherds and their flocks (1:7) and in Song 8:1 she cannot express her love for her beloved on the street as she again fears being brought to shame.

The poet recovers shamelessness for the lovers but only within their private world of love. But more than this, the poet presents the lovers as transcending beyond the innocence of the primordial garden lovers. The lovers of the Song have eaten, they both "know," their eyes are opened, they see, as has been demonstrated in the previous section, but in the Song of Songs, this "knowing" increases their passionate connection, their love and desire for each other. In the Song the lovers eat fruit, open their consciousness and love is heightened, rather than wrecked. This is not a revolution in the garden. In the Song of Songs, the whole scenario set forth in the book of origins, has become something entirely new. It is as if they have found a way back into the garden, and have eaten from the Tree of Life.

Aloneness

In the final lines of the Song of Songs the heroine is found by herself in the garden. This was in the Garden of Eden, Adam's place. In Gen 2:18 Adam is alone and narrator describes God as working to provide Adam with a companion. The poet of the Song of Songs almost seems to work inversely with Garden of Eden themes. In the story of the Song, especially in Song 8:13–14, it seems as if it is the heroine who is alone with God at creation. This has the interesting effect of echoing the lines of Proverbs (8:22) where God creates Woman Wisdom as the beginning of his works. Wisdom also

Remez-Derasha: Tracing the Contextual Environment

is a garden-dweller according to this text. Much of the language of Prov. 8:22–36 finds resonance in the Song: *The LORD created me at the beginning of His course . . . Rejoicing in His inhabited world, Finding delight with mankind.*

However, there may be a stronger theology that the poet is signifying here.[53] In the Garden of Eden, Adam was created first, in God's image, and woman created second as a helper, as the narrator delineates in Gen 2:18 [*ezer kenegdo*], and hence the history of interpretation of an ordained dependency, subservience and submission of woman, including the distancing of relation with God. Thus Paul can say in 1 Cor 11:7, *for a man indeed . . . is the image and glory of God, and the woman is the glory of man.* After the expulsion from Eden, and the words of Genesis 3:16, it is then patriarchy that defines the treatment of women throughout Torah. Through men *logos* is received at Sinai (Exod 19:15): *He said to the people, Prepare for the third day; don't approach a woman.* Through Moses the law is given (2 Chr 33:8). Through the sons of Aaron the priestly hierarchy is established (Exod 29:29). The appointed representatives of God's justice, the ones who will mete out death to those who rebel, are men: the priests, the prophets, the kings, the fathers, the brothers.

There is a mood in the Song of Songs that resists the political, religious and social power that dominates woman. And in its place, the world of women is celebrated, particularly the affirmation of life. Life is her original name (Gen 3:20): *The man named his wife Eve [Havah, life], because she was the mother of all the living.*

Along with the poet's curious exclusion of the father-figure, the ubiquitous appearances of the mother-figure, the associated imagery of birth, and the celebration of life and awakening, stages a challenge to patriarchy. Particularly with the confrontation of "death" in 8:6, the poet seems to assert that there are some *things of women* that have always already transcended the limits of patriarchy. Life and love, in the eyes of the poet, surpass the hard edge of patriarchy that is characterized in the Song as law and war. The Song juxtaposes life and death, love with power, and eros with logos. The life and love of women is better, says the poet, than power and law of men whose ultimate terminus is death (Song 8:6–7). Eros by definition evades restriction, restraint, politics and law. It is not an intrinsic element of conjugal duty. Eros' law, is that it is always already beyond law, and lies

---

53. A theology that is quite distinct from that derived from allegorical and traditional readings that would sustain and maintain a patriarchal reading.

in the realm of excess and gift. Eros is thus infra-juridicial, para-judicial, supra-judicial. Passion threatens the institution including the institution of marriage because at its core is the de-prioritization of law.[54]

Phyllis Trible engages with this notion of the transcendent *things of women* beautifully in her essay "Journey of a metaphor."[55] "Mother," a trope occurring frequently in the Song signifies love, romance, sexuality, birth, conception, nurturing and grace. The Absent Father signifies order, law, justice and death. Contrasting and elemental representations of mother-love and father-justice meet in the vignette concerning Solomon-the-wise and the two prostitutes, 1 Kgs 3:16–27. The King calls for a sword and threatens to cut the child that both women are claiming as their own, in two, at which the true mother compassionately cries: *"Please, my lord,"* . . . *"give her the live child; only don't kill it!"*

The love of a true mother in this case is her willingness to forgo justice in order for life to prevail. This mother simply wants her child to live. She is far less concerned with the need for the maintenance of the articles of law.

This theology in the Song of Songs is in good company. There is a great deal addressed in New Testament writings concerning the transcendence of life/love over justice/death: *For God so loved the world that he gave his only and unique Son* (John 3:16) and *the water I give him will become a spring of water inside him, welling up into eternal life!* (John 4:14).[56]

And triumphantly in The Epistle to the Hebrews, the mountain of doom, darkness and fire, the whirlwind, and shofar is transcended and Mount Zion appears aglow: *you have come to Mount Zion . . . and to the sprinkled blood that speaks better things than that of Hevel [Abel]. . .* (Heb 12:18–20).[57] The mention of *Hevel* [Abel] is significant and draws us back to the Genesis narrative. The sprinkled blood of *Hevel* called out from the ground for justice, the conviction of death of the one who had destroyed him (Gen 4:9-11).

Love calls for the perpetuation of life and this call has a woman's voice—the voice of the Song. And it is this particular vibrant quality that is described in the New Testament as the "better covenant" that the poet seems to suggest is hidden within the *Shulamith* of this second garden. In this eschatological garden of the Song, the heroine is alone. Perhaps the

---

54. LaCocque, "The Shulamite."

55. Trible, "Journey of a Metaphor," 31–59.

56. CJB translation.

57. Ibid.

poet imagines that she has made it past the cherubim's flame sword. Perhaps she offered herself up to it (8:6), and proving herself worthy of even the greatest sacrifice, passed through it (Isa 43:2); her vineyard now her own (8:12).[58]

> The Spirit and the Bride say, "Come!" Let anyone who hears say, "Come!" And let anyone who is thirsty come, let anyone who wishes, take the water of life as a gift (Rev 22:17).[59]

Does the poet imply that entry into this garden is only permitted to those that can transcend the patriarchal, rigid, hierarchical and unforgiving establishment of her society? The ones who enter this garden are lovers not "lawyers," friends not watchmen. They must be awakened ones and comrades. These friends and lovers must be prepared to give themselves up to a consuming fire, to look squarely at death, and choose abundant life.

OF GARDENS, CITIES, AND SHALOM

There are three broad movements in the Song—struggle, journey and *shalom*—and these separate and intersect in the thematic sites of discourse. *Shalom* or psychological rest, is signified by the garden. This is the destination or termination of struggle; the end of the journey. This is the object of the palpable yearning of the hero and heroine. Yet the *shalom* of the garden is fulfilled only in transient snatches in the text. Even the last verse of the Song of Songs does not present the lovers together in the garden. They are still running towards it, trying to enter it, wanting to stay in it but always somehow apart. *Shalom* in the Song is never complete or never remains complete. Aligning the text of the Song with the Garden of Eden texts illuminates underlying possibilities as to the poet's intent.

In the Garden of Eden texts the story progresses through various scenes, from Adam alone in the garden, to the scene when he first encounters Eve, and then the scene of Genesis 3 where crisis means that the garden is forever lost. In Gen 4, the couple's son, a killer, goes on to construct the first city (Gen 4:19–24). "City" could be seen as the antithesis of the Garden; the replacement dwelling place; the place of the knowing of good and evil.

---

58. Note Walsh, *Exquisite Desire*, 131, on the significance of 8:12, *my vineyard is my own*.

59. NRSV.

Earthing the Cosmic Queen

The Song of Songs could be said to have an anti-urban mood particularly in those night-time passages featuring the heroine alone, but also in the prioritising of love scenes in garden, field and wilderness.[60] If the poet's verse is in response to the Garden of Eden texts then there is a correlation between this anti-urban mood in the Song and the rise of cities and civilization associated with Cain, who took his own brother's life.

Ironically it is the holy city of Jerusalem that is at the centre of the Song of Songs. It is the centre of the Establishment, the Yahwistic cult, and home of the Temple. Jerusalem is a paradox in the Song. It is a city where it is dark and violent (chaps 3 and 5). Jerusalem does not live up to its name, City of Peace, in this text. On the contrary, it is the heroine who describes herself as a city of peace (8:10) replete with walls and towers. *Shulamith* itself is a moniker that stands for peace.

The Song attributes itself as for the "one to whom peace belongs"; *Shlomo* [lit. "his peace"] features several times. *Shlomo* is strongly associated with Jerusalem. This city was his capital and the sacred temple there was built by him. But this is also a paradox because in the Song of Songs he may be represented as a fool, who has no peace and tries to buy love (8:7, 11).

In the implicit rejection of the holy city and setting it up as a sinister foil, the poet seems to subvert the values and priorities of her society. The poet's call for deeper perception and transcendence of law and death is incendiary. The poet calls not for revolution but evolution[61] in the mind of the reader. Once again this prophetess seems to foretell New Testament theological developments: *the hour is coming when you will worship . . . neither on this mountain nor in Jerusalem* (John 4:21).[62]

---

60. The *shomrim* in the streets of the city are key antagonists in the Song, see chap. 5 and chap. 3. These do not belong to the light, but to darkness.

61. The theology espoused in the Song of Songs seems ahead of its time. The concept of life and love above justice/death seems easily oriented in New Testament writings. For this reason, I call the poetess' message evolutionary. I believe she has transformed the theology of her time into something new and something better.

62. NRSV translation.

A Message of Life

The Song of Songs represents a paradigm where *shalom* and paradise can be found between men and women in this life. It also cannot but help point towards the yearning for final peace and oneness with God in the next life. The Pharaohs kept poems of this genre for this very hope. The Song embraces human sexuality but also an associated and liberated spirituality. The poet's song is startling in the way it subtly subverts patriarchal institutions of law. The poet's lovers transcend Moses.

The symbolism of this story is strikingly relevant to the text's first audiences in Ancient Israel precisely because this symbolism seems to suggest a rewriting and retelling of the biblical story of beginnings that these audiences knew well, even off by heart. The Song is replete with Garden of Eden symbols and imagery that have been reworked and re-embedded with new meaning. The desire that was the undoing of the primeval couple becomes the salvation of the couple in the Song, particularly the heroine. The old story that led to death is reworked as a story that leads to life and life more abundant. For the poet this poetry is possibly the most advantageous way that she could communicate this innovative, creative and transformative message of life.

Conclusion

In this book we have read the scroll of the Song of Songs via the lens of Relevance Theory: a theory that represents contemporary understanding of the nature of language. Using *pardes*, the acronym for a medieval Jewish hermeneutic, we have surveyed the impact of Relevance on the Song of Songs as a whole. In *Peshat* we have studied the surface level of the Song through a pragmatic analysis of discourse and in *Remez-Derasha* we have traced, via hints and echoes, several motifs transparently operating in the Song to their provenance in *Gan' Eden,* the Hebrew creation myth.

We have considered evidence within the text from the background of Relevance Theory, that the poet of the Song of Songs is delivering a consistent message concerning the nature of desire and love as it engages with the socio-religious and patriarchal context of Ancient Israel. The analysis of the discourse of the Song suggests that the poet's crisis has led her to innovate the creation-garden paradigm positing a new relational ethic and theology.

This book contributes to a focussed study of Relevance Theory and ways it might open up the ancient biblical text but also serves as a platform for new directions. Questions at the level of *Remez* and *Derasha* still require attention. The garden paradigm is the primary motif engaged in the Song of Songs, however there are others. *The Wilderness* is a prominent feature in the Song which deserves further analysis. The poet crafts strong implicatures that evoke for the reader a connection with paradigms and images and personalities of the journeying period of Israel (from Abraham to Moses) which saw the institutions of ritual, priesthood, the *Mishkan* and temple. The poet also draws the reader to connect with images of coming up into the Promised Land, the establishment of Jerusalem and the Temple, and the associated glory of the Davidide Kingship over the tribes. These implicatures signalled in the Song need to be properly traced and unpacked for their wealth of meaning.

Earthing the Cosmic Queen

Further at the level of *Derasha*, how does the voice of the Song orient within the canon beyond the Garden of Eden, especially considering her strong and challenging message of love and life? Is this text the *Holy of Holies* as Rabbi Akiba claimed? The scroll of the Song of Songs engages the theology of sexuality in ways that purely naturalistic or allegorical readings do not adequately explain. Writers such as David Carr and Peter Black among others are beginning to address these.[1] The voice in the Song needs to be heard anew in the theology of sexuality in the New Testament. How does she align with New Testament writings that seem to suppress the body and sexuality in preference to a pure, cerebral spirituality?

The Song of Songs has the potential to profoundly impact the theology of sexuality and gender if these messages uncovered here are further explored. Furthermore there is a deep theology at work in the Song, that might be the hermeneutical work represented by the category of *Sohd*, that is the deep and profound reading. This still and quiet voice in the Song of Songs seems to align compatibly with other voices calling for love, life and peace in the Prophetic and also in New Testament writings, while also engaging and challenging other voices in the same canon that call for justice, war and death. This voice of life in the Song of Songs has a prophetic quality itself, and seems to speak to a reality beyond its time and place; a reality that contemporary society still has not realised.

Finally, there is the prospect of understanding the way that the Song of Songs from within the canon of biblical literature, and with respect to her distinctiveness, engages and impacts the theology of God. The poet's view of God through the framework of her love song is refreshing and revolutionary. This is a God that is neither distant, nor simplistic, nor purely cerebral, but may be glimpsed in the exhilaration of human love, and in the earthiest of human pleasures.

---

1. David Carr particularly in this regard Carr, *The Erotic Word*; Karl Barth cited in Ricoeur, "The Nuptial Metaphor," 296; and Bell, *Sex God*.

אל-גנת אגוז

ירדתי

לרעות באבי הנחל

לראות הפרחה הגפן

הנצו נרמנים

לא ידעתי

נפשי שמתני

מרכבות עמי נדיב

Into the grove of walnuts
    I descended
        To see the lushness of the streams
        To see the budding vines
        To see the bursting pomegranate flowers
. . . Before I knew it
    my passion set me
        in the chariots of a Prince

Song 6:11–12

Bibliography

Abegg, Martin Jr., Peter Flint, and Eugene Ulrich. *The Dead Sea Scrolls Bible*. New York: HarperSanFrancisco, 1999.
Alexander, Philip S. "From Poetry to Historiography: The Image of the Hasmoneans in Targum Canticles and the Question of the Targum's Provenance and Date." *Journal for the Study of the Pseudepigrapha* 19 (1999) 103–28.
Almazán García, E. M. "Dwelling in Marble Halls: A Relevance-Theoretic Approach to Intertextuality in Translation." *Revista Alicantina de Estudios Ingleses* 14 (2001) 7–19.
Amit, Yairah. *Reading Biblical Narratives: Literary Criticism and the Hebrew Bible*. Minneapolis: Fortress, 2001.
Aseidu, F. B. A. "Illocutionary Acts and the Uncanny: On Nicholas Wolterstorff's Idea of Divine Discourse." *HeyJ* 42 (2001) 283–310.
———. "The Song of Songs and the Ascent of the Soul: Ambrose, Augustine and the Language of Mysticism." *Vigiliae Christianae* 55 (2001) 299–317.
Austin, J. L. *How to Do Things with Words*. Edited by J. O. Urmson and Marina Sbisà. 2nd ed. Cambridge, MA: Harvard University Press, 1975.
Barr, James. *The Semantics of Biblical Language*. London: Oxford University Press, 1961.
Bell, Rob. *Sex God: Exploring the Endless Connections between Sexuality and Spirituality*. Grand Rapids: Zondervan, 2007.
Beaugrande, Robert de, and Wolfgang Dressler. *Introduction to Text Linguistics*. Longman Linguistics Library 26. London: Longman, 1981.
Berg, J. "The Relevant Relevance." *Journal of Pragmatics* 16 (1991) 411–25.
Bird, Phyllis A. *Missing Persons and Mistaken Identities*. Minneapolis: Fortress, 1997.
Black, Fiona C. *The Artifice of Love: Grotesque Bodies in the Song of Songs*. London: T. & T. Clark, 2009.
———. "Beauty or the Beast? The Grotesque Body in the Song of Songs." *Biblical Interpretation* 8/3 (2000) 303–23.
Black, Peter. "The Broken Wings of Eros: Christian Ethics and the Denial of Desire." *Theological Studies* 64/1 (2003) 106.
Blakemore, D. *Semantic Constraints on Relevance*. Oxford: Blackwell, 1987.
———. *Understanding Utterances*. Oxford: Blackwell, 1992.
Bloch, Ariel, and Chana Bloch. *The Song of Songs: A New Translation with Introduction and Commentary*. Berkeley: University of California Press, 1995.
Blumenthal, David R. "Where God Is Not: The Book of Esther and Song of Songs." *Judaism* 44/1 (1995) 80–90.

Bibliography

Boer, Roland. "The Second Coming: Repetition and Insatiable Desire in the Song of Songs." *Biblical Interpretation* 8/3 (2000) 276–301.
Bowker, John. *The Targums and Rabbinic Literature*. Cambridge: Cambridge University Press, 1969.
Brenner, Athalya. "The Food of Love: Gendered Food and Food Imagery in the Song of Songs." *Semeia* 86 (1999) 101–12.
———. "Gazing Back at the Shulammite, Yet Again." *Biblical Interpretation* 11/3–4 (2003) 296–300.
———. "'My' Song of Songs." In *The Song of Songs: A Feminist Companion to the Bible* 2, edited by Athalya Brenner and Carol R. Fontaine, 154–68. Sheffield, UK: Sheffield Academic Press, 2000.
———. *The Song of Songs*. Edited by R. N. Whybray. Old Testament Guides. Sheffield, UK: JSOT, 1989.
Brenner, Athalya, and Carol R. Fontaine, eds. *The Song of Songs: A Feminist Companion to the Bible* 2. Sheffield, UK: Sheffield Academic Press, 2000.
Briggs, Richard. *Words in Action: Speech Act Theory and Biblical Interpretation*. London: T. & T. Clark, 2003.
Brown, Gillian, and George Yule. *Discourse Analysis*. Cambridge: Cambridge University Press, 1983.
Bullis, Ronald K. "Biblical Tantra: Lessons in Sacred Sexuality." *Theology and Sexuality* 9 (1998) 101–16.
Burrus, Virginia, and Stephen D. Moore. "Unsafe Sex: Feminism, Pornography and the Song of Songs." *Biblical Interpretation* 11/3–4 (2003) 24–52.
Bynon, Theodora. *Historical Linguistics*. Cambridge: Cambridge University Press, 1977.
Cainon, Ivory J. "An Analogy of the Song of Songs and Genesis Chapters Two and Three." *Scandinavian Journal of the Old Testament* 14/2 (2000) 220–60.
Campbell, Joseph, and Bill Moyers. *The Power of Myth*. New York: Anchor, 1991.
Carr, David. *The Erotic Word: Sexuality, Spirituality, and the Bible*. Oxford: Oxford University Press, 2003.
Carston, R., and S. Uchida. *Relevance Theory: Applications and Implications*. Amsterdam: John Benjamin, 1998.
Charry, Ellen T. "Female Sexuality as an Image of Empowerment: Two Models." *Saint Luke's Journal of Theology* 30/3 (1987) 201–18.
Chave, Peter. "Towards a Not Too Rosy Picture of the Song of Songs." *Feminist Theology: The Journal of the Britain and Ireland School of Feminist Theology* 18 (1998) 41–54.
Chomsky, Noam. *Language and Mind*. New York: Harcourt Brace Jovanovich, 1972.
Cixous, Hélène. *Three Steps on the Ladder of Writing*. Translated by Sarah Cornell and Susan Sellers. New York: Columbia University Press, 1993.
Clark, David K. *To Know and Love God: Method for Theology*. Foundations of Evangelical Theology. Wheaton, IL: Crossway, 2003.
Clines, David. *I, He, We, and They: A Literary Approach to Isaiah 53*. Sheffield, UK: Sheffield Academic Press, 1976.
———. "Why Is There a Song of Songs and What Does It Do to You If You Read It?" In *Interested Parties: The Ideology of Writers and Readers of the Hebrew Bible*, 94–121. JSOTSup. 205. Sheffield, UK: Sheffield Academic Press, 1995.
Coward, Harold G., and K. Kunjunni Raja, eds. *The Philosophies of the Grammarians*. Vol. 5, *Encyclopedia of Indian Philosophies*. Delhi: Motilal Banarsidass, 1983.

Bibliography

Croatto, J. Severino. *Biblical Hermeneutics: Toward a Theory of Reading as the Production of Meaning.* New York: Orbis, 1987.

Crystal, David. *The Cambridge Encyclopedia of Language.* 2nd ed. Cambridge: Cambridge University Press, 1997.

———. "Pragmatics." In *The Cambridge Encyclopedia of Language,* 120–23. Cambridge: Cambridge University Press, 1997.

Culler, J. *The Pursuit of Signs: Semiotics, Literature, Deconstruction.* Ithaca, NY: Cornell University Press, 1981.

Dan, Joseph. "The Religious Experience of the Merkavah." In *Jewish Spirituality: From the Bible through the Middle Ages,* edited by Arthur Green, 289–307. London: SCM, 1989.

———. *Studies in Jewish Thought.* New York: Praeger, 1989.

Davidson, Richard. *Flame of Yahweh: Sexuality in the Old Testament.* Peabody, MA: Hendrickson, 2007.

Douglas, J. D., N. Hillyer and D. R. W. Wood, eds. *New Bible Dictionary.* Downers Grove, IL: InterVarsity, 1996.

Eisler, Riane. *Sacred Pleasure: Sex, Myth and the Politics of the Body—New Paths to Power and Love.* Sydney: Doubleday, 1996.

Elliger, K., W. Rudolph, and G. E. Weil, eds. *Biblia Hebraica Stuttgartensia.* 5th ed. Stuttgart: Deutsche Bibelgesellschaft, 1997.

Exum, J. Cheryl. "Seeing Solomon's Palanquin." *Biblical Interpretation* 11/3-4 (2003) 301–16.

———. *Song of Songs: A Commentary.* OTL. Louisville, KY: Westminster John Knox, 2005.

Falk, Marcia. *Song of Songs.* San Francisco: Harper & Row, 1990.

———. *The Song of Songs: Love Lyrics from the Bible.* Lebanon, NH: Brandeis, 2004.

Fee, Gordon D., and Douglas Stuart. *How to Read the Bible for All It's Worth.* 3rd ed. Grand Rapids: Zondervan, 2003.

Fox, Michael V. *The Song of Songs and the Ancient Egyptian Love Songs.* Madison: University of Wisconsin Press, 1985.

Gafni, Mordechai. "Homo Imaginus and the Erotics of Imagination." *Tikkun* 18/1 (2003) 54. Online: http://www.tikkun.org/article.php/JanFeb2003TOC.

Gellman, Jerome I. "Gender and Sexuality in the Garden of Eden." *Theology and Sexuality* 12/3 (2006) 319–35.

Gill, John. *An Exposition of the Old Testament.* Eighteenth Century Collections [online]. London: John Gill & George Keith, 1763–65.

Gordis, Robert. *The Song of Songs.* New York: Jewish Theological Seminary, 1954.

Gotz, Ignacio L. "Sex and Mysticism." *Crosscurrents* 54 (2004) 7–22.

Graham, Elaine. "Towards a Theology of Desire." *Theology and Sexuality* 1 (1994) 13–30.

Grice, Paul. *Studies in the Way of Words.* Cambridge, MA: Harvard University Press, 1991.

Gutt, E. A. *Relevance Theory: A Guide to Successful Communication in Translation.* Dallas: Summer Institute of Linguistics, 1992.

Hagedorn, Anselm C. "Of Foxes and Vineyards: Greek Perspectives on the Song of Songs." *Vetus Testamentum* 53/3 (2003) 337–52.

Inge, William Ralph. *The Awakening of the Soul: An Introduction to Christian Mysticism.* Edited by A. F. Judd. London: A. R. Mowbray, 1959.

Jacobs, Louis. *A Concise Companion to the Jewish Religion.* Oxford: Oxford University Press, 1999.

Bibliography

Katsanis, Bobbi Dykema. "Meeting in the Garden: Intertextuality with the Song of Songs in Holbein's Noli Me Tangere1." *Interpretation* 61/4 (2007) 402–18.

Keel, Othmar. *The Song of Songs: A Continental Commentary*. Translated by Frederick J. Gaiser. Minneapolis: Fortress, 1994.

Klangwisan, Yael. *Jouissance: A Cixousian Encounter with the Song of Songs*. Sheffield, UK: Sheffield Phoenix, 2014.

LaCocque, André. "The Shulamite." In *Thinking Biblically: Exegetical and Hermeneutical Studies*, edited by André LaCocque and Paul Ricoeur, 235–64. Chicago: University of Chicago Press, 1998.

Landy, Francis. *Beauty and the Enigma and Other Essays on the Hebrew Bible*. New York: Continuum, 2001.

———. "The Song of Songs." In *The Literary Guide to the Bible*, edited by Robert Alter and Frank Kermode, 305–19. Cambridge, MA: Harvard University Press, 1987.

———. "The Song of Songs and the Garden of Eden." *Journal of Biblical Literature* 98 (1979) 513–28.

———. "Two Versions of Paradise." In *The Song of Songs: A Feminist Companion to the Bible*, edited by Athalya Brenner, 129–42. Sheffield, UK: Sheffield Academic Press, 1993.

Langermann, Y. Tzvi. "Saving the Soul by Knowing the Soul: A Medieval Yemeni Interpretation of Song of Songs." *The Journal of Jewish Thought and Philosophy* 12/2 (2003) 147–66.

Lehrman, S. M. "The Song of Songs." In *The Five Megilloth*, edited by A. Cohen, x–32. London: Soncino, 1974.

Long, Gary Alan. "A Lover, Cities, and Heavenly Bodies: Co-Text and the Translation of Two Similes in Canticles." *Journal of Biblical Literature* 115 (1996) 703–9.

Longman, Tremper, III. *Song of Songs*. New International Commentary on the Old Testament. Grand Rapids: Eerdmans, 2001.

Marks, John H., and Robert M. Good, eds. *Love and Death in the Ancient Near East: Essays in Honour of Marvin H. Pope*. Guilford, CT: Four Quarters, 1987.

Matt, Daniel C. *The Essential Kabbalah: The Heart of Jewish Mysticism*. San Francisco: HarperSanFrancisco, 1996.

McIntosh, Mark A. *Mystical Theology*. Malden, MA: Blackwell, 1998.

Menn, Esther M. "Thwarted Metaphors: Complicating the Language of Desire in the Targum of the Song of Songs." *Journal for the Study of Judaism* 34/3 (2003) 238–73.

Meyers, Carol L. *Discovering Eve: Ancient Israelite Women in Context*. Oxford: Oxford University Press, 1988.

Millgram, Abraham. *Jewish Worship*. 2nd ed. Philadelphia: Jewish Publication Society of America, 1971.

Molé, Phil. "Occam's Razor Cuts Both Ways." *Skeptic* 10/1 (2003) 40–48.

Moore, Stephen D. "The Song of Songs in the History of Sexuality." *Church History* 69/2 (2000) 328–49.

Munro, Jill M. *Spikenard and Saffron: A Study in the Poetic Language of the Song of Songs*. JSOTSup 203. Sheffield, UK: Sheffield Academic Press, 1995.

Murphy, Roland. *The Song of Songs: A Commentary on the Canticles or the Song of Songs*. Hermeneia. Minneapolis: Augsburg Fortress, 1990.

Niditch, Susan. *Oral World and Written Word: Ancient Israelite Literature*. London: SPCK, 1997.

Bibliography

Ostriker, Alicia. "A Holy of Holies: The Song of Songs as Countertext." In *The Song of Songs*, edited by Athalya Brenner and Carole R. Fontaine, 36–54. Sheffield, UK: Sheffield Academic Press, 2000.

Patmore, Hector. "'The Plain and Literal Sense': On Contemporary Assumptions about the Song of Songs." *Vetus Testamentum* 56/2 (2006) 239–50.

Pattemore, Stephen. *The People of God in the Apocalypse: Discourse, Structure and Exegesis.* Cambridge: Cambridge University Press, 2004.

———. "Relevance Theory, Intertexuality and the Book of Revelation." *UBS Bulletin: Current Trends in Scripture Translation* 194/195 (2002) 43–60.

Pecknold, C. C. "The Readable City and the Rhetoric of Excess: A Reading of the Song of Songs." *Cross currents* 52/4 (2003) 516–20.

Peterson, Eugene, ed. *The Message: The Bible in Contemporary Language.* Colorado Springs: NavPress, 2003.

Pope, Marvin H. *Song of Songs: A New Translation with Introduction and Commentary.* Anchor Bible. Garden City, NY: Doubleday, 1977.

Ricoeur, Paul. "The Nuptial Metaphor." In *Thinking Biblically: Exegetical and Hermeneutical Studies*, edited by André LaCocque and Paul Ricoeur, 265–303. Chicago: University of Chicago Press 1998.

Ross, Allen P. *Introducing Biblical Hebrew.* Grand Rapids: Baker Academic, 2001.

Russell, Bertrand. "On Denoting." *Mind* 14/56 (1905) 479–93.

Russell, D. S. *Divine Disclosure.* Minneapolis: Fortress, 1992.

Saussure, Ferdinand de. *Course in General Linguistics.* Translated by W. Baskin. Glasgow: FontanaCollins, 1977.

———. *Course in General Linguistics.* Translated by Roy Harris. Open Court Classics. Peru, IL: Open Court, 1986.

Scherman, Nosson, ed. *Tanach.* The Stone edition. Artscroll. New York: Mesorah, 1996.

———. *Zohar: The Book of Splendour.* New York: Schocken, 1949.

Scott, David C. "Radha in the Erotic Play of the Universe." *Christian Century* 3 (1995) 239–42.

Searle, John R. *Expression and Meaning: Studies in the Theory of Speech Acts.* Cambridge: Cambridge University Press, 1979.

———. *Intentionality: An Essay in the Philosophy of Mind.* Cambridge: Cambridge University Press, 1983.

———. *Speech Acts: An Essay in the Philosophy of Language.* Cambridge: Cambridge University Press, 1970.

Sembene, Ousmane, dir. *Moolaade.* Senegal: Madman Entertainment, 2004.

Sharaby, Rachel. "The Bride's Henna Ritual: Symbols, Meanings and Changes." *Nashim* 11 (Spring 2006) 11–42.

Shirazi, Faegheh S. "The Sofreh: Comfort and Community among Women in Iran." *Iranian Studies* 38/2 (2005) 293–309.

Sperber, Dan, and Dierdre Wilson. "Précis of Relevance: Communication and Cognition." *Behavioural and Brain Sciences* 10 (1987) 697–754.

———. *Relevance: Communication and Cognition.* 2nd ed. Oxford: Blackwell, 1995.

Sperling, H. "Jewish Mysticism." In *Aspects of the Hebrew Genius*, edited by Leon Simon, 145–76. London: Routledge, 1910.

Suderman, W. Derek. "Modest or Magnificent? Lotus versus Lily in Canticles." *The Catholic Biblical Quarterly* 65 (2005) 42–58.

Bibliography

Sviri, Sara. "The Song of Songs: Eros and the Mystical Quest." In *Jewish Explorations of Sexuality*, edited by Jonathan Magonet, 41–50. Providence, RI: Berghahn, 1994.

Thiselton, Anthony C. "Semantics and New Testament Interpretation." In *New Testament Interpretation: Essays on Principles and Methods*, edited by I. Howard Marshall, 75–104. Exeter: Paternoster, 1985.

Thomas, Robert L. "Modern Linguistics versus Traditional Hermeneutics." *Master's Seminary Journal* 14/1 (2003) 23–45.

Toorn, K. van der, B. Becking, and Pieter W. Van Der Horst. *Dictionary of Deities and Demons in the Bible*. Leiden: Brill, 1995.

Trible, Phyllis. "Depatriachalizing in Biblical Interpretation." *Journal of the American Academy of Religion* 41 (1973) 30–48.

———. "Journey of a Metaphor." In *God and the Rhetoric of Sexuality*, 31–59. Philadelphia: Fortress, 1978.

———. "Love's Lyrics Redeemed." In *God and the Rhetoric of Sexuality*, 144–65. Philadelphia: Fortress, 1978.

Vanhoozer, Kevin. "From Speech Acts to Scripture Acts: The Covenant of Discourse and the Discourse of the Covenant." In *After Pentecost: Language and Biblical Interpretation*, edited by C. Bartholomew, C. Greene, and K. Möller, 1–49. Grand Rapids: Zondervan, 2001.

Walsh, Carey Ellen. *Exquisite Desire: Religion, the Erotic, and the Song of Songs*. Minneapolis: Fortress, 2000.

Ward, Graham. "The Erotics of Redemption: After Karl Barth." *Theology and Sexuality* 8 (1998) 52–72.

Watts, Rikk E. "Making Sense of Genesis." The American Scientific Affiliation: Science in Christian Perspective. 2002. Online: http://www.asa3.org/ASA/topics/Bible-Science/6-02Watts.html.

Wendland, Ernst, R. "On the Relevance of 'Relevance Theory' for Bible Translation." *Bible Translator* 47/1 (1996) 126–37.

———. "Seeking the Path through a Forest of Symbols: A Figurative and Structural Survey of the Song of Songs." *Journal of Translation and Textlinguistics* 7 (1995) 13–59.

Werblowsky, Zwi. "Jewish Mysticism." In *The Jewish World*, edited by Elie Kedourie, 217–23. London: Thames & Hudson, 1979.

White, Hugh C. "Desire and Promise in Genesis." *Word and World* 14 (1994) 178–85.

Wilson, Dierdre, and Dan Sperber. "Relevance Theory." In *Handbook of Pragmatics*, edited by G. Ward and L. Horn, 607–32. Oxford: Blackwell, 2004.

Wittgenstein, Ludwig. *Tractatus Logico-Philosophicus*. Translated by David Pears and Brian McGuinness. New York: Humanities, 1961.

www.ingramcontent.com/pod-product-compliance
Lightning Source LLC
Chambersburg PA
CBHW050815160426
43192CB00010B/1768